A Doctor in the Forest

A Doctor in the Forest

By Bill Tandy.

DOUGLAS McLEAN
THE FOREST BOOKSHOP

First published in Great Britain by

DOUGLAS McLEAN

at

THE FOREST BOOKSHOP,

32 Market Place, Coleford, Glos. GL16 8AA.

First Published August 1978

Reprinted August 1978

and July 1979

© W. H. TANDY 1978

ISBN 0 9505926 1 7

Type set in 12 pt. Perpetua

BILL TANDY

A
DOCTOR
IN
THE
FOREST

Illustrated By
DOUG EATON

ACKNOWLEDGEMENT

I am indebted to Mr Patrick Harvey of Yorkley for help with the chapter on his father F. W. Harvey, the Forest poet, and to Mr Tom Bright of Coleford for his encouragement and advice.

John Helps a wer an honest mon;
 The perry that a made
Wer crunched vrom purs as honest
 As ever tree displayed.

John Helps a wer an honest mon;
 The dumplings that a chewed
Wer made vrom honest apples
 As Autumn ever growed.

John Helps a wer an honest mon;
 And I be sorry a's dead.
Perry and honest men be scarce
 These days, 'tiz zed.

                         F. W. Harvey.

CONTENTS

Foreword

I came to live in the Royal Forest of Dean nearly forty years ago. Previously I had spent some years living and working as a surgeon in charge of a Quaker Hospital in that part of mid-India where the sacred Narbadda river flows on its long journey to the Gulf of Cambray. It was a pastoral countryside of innumerable villages, the real India. There was much I missed when I left India. I missed the peasant people travelling in their bullock-carts and ploughing their fields with the help of their oxen. I missed seeing the village women walking with elegant deportment, dressed in brightly coloured saris, with their water-pots on their heads, to the well. I missed the vivacious laughing Indian village children. I missed the festivals, especially Divali, the autumn festival of lights, when their houses were lit up at night by myriads of tiny lamps. To the north of where I was living were the Vindhya range of hills, and the Satpura range was to the south. Those hills were jungle country, Kipling's jungle. They were the homeland of the Gonds, a primitive Dravidian people, animists who peopled the trees, the hills and the rivers with spirits. I missed meeting them in those jungle hills where lurked the tiger, the panther, the ugly hyena and the graceful leaping deer. Laughter and song and the dance filled their leisure hours. I missed hearing the throb of their drums as they danced their ancient dances, conjuring up within themselves the ancestral spirits of their past. I missed seeing the Gond women in their brick-red saris and tight green bodices, with large metal anklets that jangled as they walked, carrying large bundles of wood on their heads. With regal grace they picked their way along the forest paths. The jungle and the villages of India had fascinated and capitvated me as they have done for many an Englishman over the years.

I had to leave it all behind for ever. I had to leave the Gonds and the village folk I had grown so fond of. I left behind a large part of my heart. Instead I came to live in the Forest of Dean, exchanging the pepal, the teak, the banyan and the mohar trees for the oaks and elms and beeches and conifers. I missed seeing the black-faced and the red-faced chattering monkeys swinging and gambolling in the trees and the wild screeching peacocks perched on the branches. I exchanged the sacred Narbadda river for the Severn and the Wye. I exchanged the azure blue of the linseed fields of mid-India for the deep blue of the English bluebells, shimmering as the sunlight comes through the fresh young beech leaves in the woods in May. I came to live and work in another forest, in that triangle of very ancient land which is enclosed between the Severn and the Wye as they meander on their way to meet each other near Chepstow. There I found another forest-dwelling people, a closed community, and I discovered that they were the last of the Ancient Britons. I settled down amongst them and many became my patients. Now in my retirement, I remember those days before the motor-car, the Welfare State and the National Health Service changed everything.

Several of my friends have encouraged me to write about what I remember of those early days when I first settled down in the Forest of Dean. This I have tried to do. The book claims no literary merit, it is not autobiographical, nor is it nostalgic. I am but gossiping about some people I knew a long time ago.

The gossip is true but their names are fictitious. Although they are no longer here I must respect them by giving them anonymity, not just on account of medical ethics, but because of the affection I have in my memory of them.

BILL TANDY,

Newland.

14th Century Free Miners Brass in Newland Church

CHAPTER ONE

The Dobunni Tribe

Lloyd George introduced the National Insurance Act in 1911. It provided manual workers, and also non manual workers earning less than £160 a year — a figure increased to £250 before I came to the Forest and in January 1942 to £420 — with free medical attention. The Act did not cover dependents. They, with everyone else did not become entitled to free medical treatment until the National Health Service was introduced in 1948. Thirty years had gone by since Lloyd George's Act, yet Arthur Jones, an elderly Forester, a miner who lived alone, could not rid himself of the idea that there was charity associated with it. Charity was something he could not accept. Each time he came to see me he would bring a small gift as

Arthur was in his late seventies. He still worked at the coal face. When I felt his pulse it was irregular and bumpy, the radial artery felt hard and beaded from impregnated chalk. I advised him a number of times that he should give up work.

"I bain't able to," he would reply, "I be savin up fer me old age."

He came into the surgery one day bringing an old lemonade bottle with a dirty label on it which contained a turbid red liquid. He put it on my desk. I picked it up and looked at it, then looked up at him. "How long have you been passing blood in your water?" I asked him. A pained and shocked expression spread across his face. "That be me special 'ome-made blackberry wine," he informed me. I never got round to sampling his wine. When I picked up the bottle something seemed to deter me from pouring any out to taste. Later Arthur was found dead in bed, having died in his sleep. He had been at work the day before, still saving up for his old age.

o   o   o

It is a far cry from the central plateau of India to that piece of England, the Forest of Dean, that lies in the angle where the rivers Severn and Wye converge, meeting at the Estuary now spanned by the Severn Bridge. I settled down there early in 1940, long before the bridge was built. The only way to cross the Estuary then was by means of a ramshackle old ferry boat operating from a dilapidated jetty. Recuperating from amoebic dysentery, malaria and an attack of polio-myelitis the life of a country G.P. Surgeon seemed to offer a suitable existence after the open-air life I had been living up-country in India. City life had no attraction.

It was an abrupt change from the mud houses of the Indian Villages to the dull grey stone dwellings of the Dean villages; from the people of the lovely Narbaada Valley to the mining communities of the beautiful Forest of Dean.

It was a move from one type of forest-dweller to another,

from the people of the lovely Narbaada Valley to the mining communities of the beautiful Forest of Dean.

It was a move from one type of forest-dweller to another, from one civilisation to another. However, they both have one thing in common. They are both ancient civilisations that have the same ancestry. Both had their origins somewhere near the Caucasus where a nomadic steppe people had learnt to tame the horse. From there the nomadic Indo-Europeans spread east towards India and west into Europe. From those that spread west the Celts emerged, extending from the Mediterranean to the most northern parts of Britain and to Ireland. The Hindu Brahmin and the Celtic Druid sprang from a common priestly caste. The Indian and the European languages, diverse as they now are, were derived from the common speech of those steppe people.

Goodness knows how many millennia ago all this happened, or how long it took. Even before it did happen Neolithic man had walked the earth for many thousand years. He erected the stones which still stand up to mystify the men of this modern age who ponder about their significance. They extend from the Shetland Isles to Stonehenge and across Europe. There is a standing stone between Coleford and the Buckstone at Staunton in the Forest of Dean, and there are the standing stones at Trelleck a few miles away across the river Wye.

The Hebridean people have a saying "When God made time He made plenty of it". He surely did!

When I settled in the Forest of Dean the miners had been there for several thousand years, a race of human moles burrowing into the earth to bring out the iron-ore and the coal. They are the descendants of a Celtic tribe, the Dobunni. The tribe once occupied a large area, its centre being between Cirencester and Chippenham, and its periphery westwards extended across the river Severn as far as the river Wye.

The Dobunni tribe fought the Roman Legions stubbornly, being the last of the ancient Britons to be subdued. Then, for three hundred years, those who lived in what is now the Forest

When they were sick in body, mind or spirit, they visited a hill overlooking the Severn Estuary on which there was a Romano-Celtic temple dedicated to the God, Nodens, a God of healing, and cast their votive offerings to him. The remains of the temple have been uncovered, and can be seen on Lord Bledisloe's estate just outside Lydney.

When the Roman Legions eventually left Britain early in the fifth century A.D., the Dobunni miners were free again. About a hundred years later a Romanised Celtic family living on the edge of the Forest of Dean near the river Severn owned some land which they farmed. They had a sixteen year old lad. One day there was a raid up the Severn estuary by barbarian Celts from Ireland. They kidnapped the lad and took him back to Ireland as a slave. Later he escaped and after various adventures arrived in Rome. There he was converted to Christianity. After preparation, training and study he returned to Ireland. He converted the Irish barbarians to Christianity. His name was Patrick.

It was not long after the Roman legions withdrew from Britain that the Dobunni tribe was fighting the Angles from across the North Sea. It was a losing battle, but those who were not exterminated retreated westwards across the Severn and waged a guerrilla war from the thickness of the Dean Forest. They maintained their freedom to work the iron-mines there, stubbornly defending their freedom. They kept what was left of their tribe intact, refusing to inter-marry with the Angles. Later they became isolated to the West by the southern end of the famous dyke, built on the orders of Offa, King of Mercia between 750 and 800 A.D., which extended from the Sedbury cliffs near Chepstow all the way to Chester, as a boundary warding off the marauding Celtic-Silures tribe from Wales. Early in the eleventh century King Canute instituted the office of Verderer to protect the forest. The Verderer's Court has functioned ever since, still sitting today at the Speech House.

The Dubonni continued mining while the Norman Kings used the Royal Forest to hunt the deer, subjecting the forest dwellers to their Forest Courts, killing and mutilating them if they broke the cruel Forest laws.

Eventually, during the last quarter of the thirteenth century, Edward the First acknowledged their rights to mine the forest. There have been free miners ever since. To be a Free Miner a man has to be born within the Hundreds of St. Briavels and to have worked a year and a day in a mine. There are Free Miners today, although their freedom is again assaulted, this time by their modern overlords, the planning bureaucrats of Gloucester's Shire Hall.

There is an emblem of their freedom in the Church of my village of Newland, the Free Miners' brass. It depicts a Miner in 14th Century costume with his pick in his hand, his hod slung over his shoulder, holding a candle between his teeth to give him his only light whilst working in the darkness of his mine. The brass was probably struck by Edward the First to confirm his assent of the mining rights of the Foresters. Edward the First's maxim was "to each his own". G. M. Trevelyan, the historian, called him "the legal minded king". What is significant about the brass is that the miner is standing *above* a knight's helmet, to establish that his rights are superior to any feudal peer or overlord. It is one of the great brasses of Britain, seven hundred years old.

The Dean Foresters became experts not only in mining but in the use of the long bow. Such was their reputation that in 1310 a hundred archers together with miners were sent by the King from the Dean Forest to help him to raise the seige of Berwick-on-Tweed. The miners dug tunnels under the defence perimeter of the town.

Oaks from the Forest of Dean were used to build the fleet that was used to defeat the Spanish Armada. Drake and Raleigh both visited the Forest while the ships were being built.

The Dean Forester is stubborn, he clings to his ancient rights, he becomes rebellious if they are threatened. He can be suspicious of any foreigner, a foreigner being anybody not born in his Forest of Dean. I was a foreigner when I settled among this he becomes rebellious if they are threatened. He can be suspicious of any foreigner, a foreigner being anybody not born in his Forest of Dean. I was a foreigner when I settled among this ancient British tribe forty years ago. It was my good fortune that they accepted me.

The Forest of Dean is very different now from what it was when I first came to live in it. The Welfare State and the motor car have seen to that. No longer is it a closed community. All the coal mines have now been closed. Light industries have taken their place. No more do men spend from middle age to old age in a dyspnoeic wheezing hell from silicosis, or cut off in middle-age from silico-tuberculosis. Silicosis was the curse of the Dean Miner when he was forced by the coal owners to bore through the silica bearing rock to reach the coal underneath.

The bitterness, born of the depression following World War One, which had bitten into the heart of his grandfather has gone. However, he cannot change his genes, his collective unconscious, or whatever it is that still makes him the stubborn, freedom-loving, independent, dryly humorous man his ancestor was. He can be led, but not driven. There are still a few of them who work underground in their own small mines. They were born to it, they will tell you.

Nowadays most of them are prepared to leave their Forest to work or settle elsewhere. They have their motor cars. They travel to France, Italy and Spain for their holidays. "Foreigners" have come to live in the Forest. There are housing estates built by the local councils or by private enterprise. The old stone cottages scattered haphazardly around the district are fast disappearing. Visitors in their cars and caravans come in their thousands every summer to share the beauty of the Forest. It is all very different from what it was forty years ago.

Working amongst them during this time I have watched an era of social history unfold. I have seen the end of the isolation of the descendants of the last of the Ancient Britons.

I can conjure up in my memory those early days when I first came to live amongst them. I can recall the tragedies and the

If you asked one of them "Are you English?" he would answer "No." If you asked him "Are you Welsh?" he would answer "No." If you then asked him "What are you?" he would answer "I be a Forester." He was right! He was not English or Welsh. Across the Severn to the east are the English, the descendants of the Angles who eliminated the members of the Celtic Dobunni tribe which once lived there. Across the Wye to the west are the Welsh, the descendants of the Silures, a different Celtic tribe.

Between the two rivers in the Forest of Dean are the descendants of all that remains of the Dobunni tribe, the "freedom fighters" who retreated into the depths of the Forest and would not be subdued.

The Descendants
of the Dobunni Tribe

George Phelps had a small holding at the back of beyond near
Oldcroft. The cottage was at the end of a long dirt track. He
owned a number of sheep which grazed freely in the forest. He
also had a pig which was his heart's delight.

I was told that when he married Grace at Viney Hill Church
and the vicar asked him, "Wilt thou have this woman to thy
wedded wife?" George replied, "I will. But I'd rather 'ave 'ad
'er sister, mind."

After they had been married for a few months Grace conceived.
George was very excited about this. They booked the district
nurse for the delivery. She worked out the expected date of
delivery for them — forty weeks from the first day of her last
menstrual period.

The day arrived, but not the baby. George came to see me at the end of the evening surgery next day.

" 'er should 'ave 'ad un yesterday, doctor," he said. I reassured him, explaining that babies often arrived a few days before or a few days after the expected date. He came again the next day, and the next, and the next, getting more and more worried and anxious that Grace was still undelivered. Then he arrived one evening in a state of great excitement to give me the good news that the baby had been born.

" 'ers 'ad un, doctor," he announced, "an' 'er didn't arf 'ave 'un quick. 'er 'ad un afore nurse got there. But I looked arter 'er. I looked arter 'er real proper. If 'erd bin me old sow I couldn't 'ave looked arter 'er better."

Tom Phipps was a miner who lived in Pillowell, a village of straggling cottages on a steep hill. He was about forty-five years old when I first met him. His wife was a couple of years or so younger. They were childless.

Tom was an expert cornet player, a member of a local band. It was a very good band and had recently entered a national band competition, reaching and winning the semi-finals. The final contest was held in London. The furthest Tom had ever been from the Forest of Dean was Gloucester. A visit to London was quite an adventure for him. I met him soon after he returned. He was disappointed that his band had not won the competition. I told him that I thought the band had done very well to be the runners up. He was not to be comforted and was very critical of London. "A daft place full of daft people," he commented.

He related how he had gone into a Lyons Corner House for a meal. "A young woman cum up ter me and sez 'What'll yer 'ave.' Two cackles and a grunt, I sez. Do you know, doctor, 'er didn't know what'd meant." I did not confess that I was ignorant as to what two cackles and a grunt were either. Later I discovered that it meant two eggs and bacon.

While travelling on a London bus a young woman wearing a rather short skirt had got in and sat opposite to him. "Every time I looked 'er way 'er pulled at 'er skirt to keep 'er knees covered. Fair got on me nerves, it did. So I leant across to 'er and said 'Don't mind me, lass, *cider* be my hobby.' 'Er didn't arf glare at me."

Soon after his visit to London a tremendous event happened in Tom's life. His wife became pregnant. Nothing would induce either of them to agree to the delivery taking place in the local hospital. They were both adamant. Tom and his father and his grandfather had been born in Pillowell. Tom's baby must be born in Pillowell. The district nurse-midwife was very apprehensive. Tom's wife was a little, thin, wiry woman well over forty years old and looked older. I appreciated Nurse Jones' apprehension and assured her that I would be available if she needed any help.

One morning, in the early hours, the telephone rang, waking me up. Tom was at the other end in a kiosk. It was quite a time before he discovered that he had to press button A after putting his money in. He had had his money returned several times after pressing button B. When he eventually got through it was to tell me that his wife was in labour and Nurse Jones wanted some help from me. I drove my car to Pillowell parking it alongside Nurse's car. In the darkness, carrying my midwifery bag, I climbed the tump to Tom's cottage.

Tom opened the door to me. He was in a state of subdued excitement mingled with anxiety and mystery. He was being kept busy supplying large quantities of hot water for Nurse Jones. I climbed the steep narrow wooden staircase to the bedroom, the smell of Dettol getting stronger as I approached the bedroom door. A fire was burning briskly in the fireplace. Nurse had a large saucepan of boiling water on it for me to sterilise my instruments in. The only illumination was from an oil lamp. Tom's wife was lying on the bed looking tired and wan. "She's been fully dilated for over an hour, Doctor," Nurse said, "but she's too tired to push down any more. I think it needs helping out." I agreed with her.

I put the forceps in the saucepan and got an anaesthetic mask and a large piece of gamgee tissue and a bottle of chloroform out of my bag. The fire and the paraffin lamp precluded the use of inflammable ether. Nitrous oxide gas and oxygen had not yet arrived on the domiciliary obstetric scene. I anaesthetised the patient and then handed her over to Nurse with instructions to keep her chin up. I scrubbed my hands in the Dettol solution nurse had prepared for me in a wash-hand basin. Then I applied the forceps and gently lifted out the baby.

It was rather a puny boy, weighing five and a half pounds, but it cried lustily as soon as it was delivered. Nurse put the anaesthetic mask and the gamgee tissue aside and took charge of the baby as soon as the umbilical cord had been divided and ligatured, while I dealt with the placenta. The patient came out of the anaesthetic, was given an injection of ergometrine, and told that she had a son. Nurse shouted the news downstairs to Tom. The baby was washed, then reverently peeped at by an awed Tom. The mother was cleaned up, made comfortable, given a cup of tea while I packed up my bag. Everyone felt relieved. All had gone off satisfactorily, which was just as well, as in those days there was no flying squad, no national blood-transfusion service.

Nurse and I went downstairs with our bags. Tom had made a pot of tea for us. "I've made your tea specially strong, doctor," he said. It was strong. It was also tepid, as there was more whisky than tea in the mug.

There were feeding difficulties. Tom's wife was unable to feed the baby herself. She could not produce enough milk, which was not surprising considering her age. Cow's milk, national dried and various proprietary brands were all tried.

I met Tom when the baby was about six weeks old. I asked him how the infant was doing. "Doctor," he said, "ever since we put 'im on that there ostrich's milk 'im 'asn't looked back." I asked him if the baby cried a lot. "Oh! 'Im 'ollers a bit at times," replied Tom, "but we git 'is wind up like as 'ow the nurse showed us, then we put 'im on the end of the bed an' un da zoon drop awf."

o o o

Somebody had slipped a note under the surgery door. It read, "George is ill." That was all — no signature, no address, no date. "I wonder which George that is," I thought, "I hope he hasn't got an acute appendix."

A few days later I was driving down Fetter Hill, or Futtr'l as the Foresters call it, finishing my rounds. "I'll just pop in and see how old Hubert Thomas is, I haven't seen him lately," I said to myself.

Hubert was a retired stone-mason, a widower who lived with his middle-aged bachelor son. I was always a bit worried about him because he had the largest hernia I have ever seen. Most of his small and large intestine and his omentum lived in it. No truss could possibly have controlled that hernia. He had made a canvas bag for it, which he kept suspended by means of a belt slung over his shoulder.

The only other lump in that area of human anatomy that I have seen which was larger than Hubert's hernia belonged to a chap in India named Buddhu. His lump, however, was a hydrocele, not a hernia. Buddhu had made himself a small wheelbarrow on which he would place his hydrocele in order to get around. After a great deal of persuasion he had agreed to surgery. When he went back to his village without his lump, and carrying his wheelbarrow under his arm, the astonishment of the villagers was terrific. But I think they felt sort of cheated. The village was never quite the same again without Buddhu trundling his hydrocele along in the wheelbarrow.

Hubert's hernia was another problem altogether. It was beyond surgery at his age, and he had bad chronic bronchitis from working in stone dust for so many years. Anyhow, nobody could ever have persuaded Hubert to have an operation. His obstinacy was of a different order from Buddhu's.

Hubert was busy working in his garden when I called. He watched me as I unlatched the gate and walked over to him. I received no welcoming smile as was usual. He glowered at me. "Good morning, Hubert," I said as I reached the row of cabbages he was working on. "Why didn't you come and see my George when he was bad?" he growled back at me. "I didn't know he had been ill," I said. "I sent you a note," said Hubert.

Then I remembered the piece of paper which somebody had shoved under the surgery door some days previously. I felt I should defend myself against this accusation of professional negligence. "You only wrote 'George is ill,'" I said, "you gave no address. How was I to know which George it was?" "You bloody well know my George," said Hubert, "you bloody well know." "How is he now?" I asked, in an attempt to mollify him. "Went back to work this morning," he replied, "but he was proper bad with diarrhoea he was."

I did not remark that the lack of hygiene in their kitchen had probably been the cause of George's affliction. That would only have added fuel to the fire. "Next time you want a visit from me put your address on the note," I said. "You know my George," said Hubert, "you bloody well know."

I left the garden feeling rather unjustly done by. Hubert was usually so very affable and chatty. He had boasted so many times to me about how he had made the crazy pavement on Selfridge's roof-garden that I had begun to doubt the truth of it. "Only Forest of Dean stone was good enough for Selfridge's," he said, "sent all the way from London for it they did." Then he would invariably add, "Takes a crazy man to lay a crazy pavement."

Hubert's hernia killed him in the end. He did not die from any of the usual complications of a hernia, not Hubert. One day a passing motorist called at the surgery and asked me to go up to Fetter Hill urgently. George met me at the garden gate. "He's in the pig stye," he said, "the old sow butted him on his rupture and he collapsed. I think he is dead."

I went into the pig-stye and there was Hubert lying dead in the muck on the pig-stye floor. "I'm afraid he's dead," I said to George, "I expect he died from the shock." I had to report his death to the Coroner. That would have pleased old Hubert, would have made him feel important.

25

My predecessor in the practice had done his own dispensing. I had had no experience in pharmacy when I arrived at Parkend from India. When I first saw the little dispensary I looked apprehensively at the rows of Winchester bottles of various mixtures, the bottles of tonics, elixirs, tinctures, a large bottle of Linctus Gee, tins containing powders, jars of greasy ointments, the glass measures and the apothecary's scales. I did not relish the prospect of dispensing for the patients. Anyhow it seemed to be an awful waste of a doctor's time mixing up bottles of medicine.

The second day after I started working in the practice Ted Hughes came in. He had been to see me the previous day complaining of indigestion for which I had mixed up a bottle of medicine. He was very polite. He put the bottle on my desk and said, "I'm sure this is an excellent bottle of medicine, doctor, but I can't make it pour."

The next patient was not so polite. He had also been to see me the day before. He had been wearing his best suit as he was going to a friend's wedding that day. He had put his bottle of medicine in the pocket of his jacket. About ten minutes after leaving the surgery the cork had blown off erupting a frothing, creamy, white sticky substance which had made havoc of his jacket. I decided I must get somebody to do the dispensing for me.

I was fortunate in obtaining the services of an excellent young woman, a Miss Richards, who had had previous dispensing experience. During the time I had to wait for her to take over her duties all the patients were given a mixture of rhubarb and soda, known as Mist. Rhei. Co. There were two Winchesters of it in the dispensary already made up in concentrated form. All I had to do was to shake up a Winchester of it, pour some into a bottle, add water, and stick on a label which read, "One tablespoonful three times a day after meals. Shake the bottle." I had remembered what my old chief had said in one of his less serious moods. "I give Mist. Rhei. Co. to patients when I know what is the matter with them. I give

Mist. Rhei. Co. to patients when I don't know what is the matter with them. And I give Mist. Rhei. Co. to patients when I just don't care a damn what's the matter with them. What is important is not what you prescribe but how you prescribe it."

When my mother was sent by her doctor for a consultation with him he prescribed Mist. Rhei. Co. for her. He was a bit cross with me when I asked him to which category my mother belonged.

Mist. Rhei. Co. was most popular with the patients. Ted Hughes loved it when I gave him some in exchange for the bottle of medicine which would not pour. He kept coming back for more. He was a tall, upright, lean active mean with a healthy complexion, an open face, and a neatly trimmed white moustache. He was eighty-five years old and looked sixty. When I asked him his age I was surprised how young he looked and told him so. That pleased him greatly. He drew himself up to his full height, expanded his chest, and said, "Yes, Doctor, I be eighty-five. And full of vigour. And I can still prove my manhood. Mind you, Doctor, it takes me longer than it used to." Then he added with a wistful smile, "But I don't begrudge the time."

As a medical student I had always smoked a pipe. When I started doing resident hospital jobs life was so hectic that there was no time to enjoy or finish a pipe. I got hooked onto cigarettes. When I went to Parkend I was smoking fifty or more a day. One day I decided I must stop. With great resolution I threw away what cigarettes I had.

Next morning the nicotine withdrawal symptoms were awful. I did a busy morning surgery having itched agonisingly for a cigarette after breakfast. I was edgy, irritable and bad tempered with each patient who came in to see me. Ted Hughes arrived for a bottle of Mist. Rhei. Co. "You're a bit crotchety this morning, aren't you, doctor," he remarked. "Yes," I said, "I'm afraid I am. I've just given up smoking cigarettes."

I struggled through the remainder of the patients trying unsuccessfully to keep the withdrawal symptoms under control. The last patient to come in was Ted Hughes again. He did not say a word. He just walked up to my desk, put a packet of twenty Players on it, and walked out." I dived for the packet, feverishly opening it with shaking fingers. I decided there and then that Ted Hughes was a wiser man than me. In later years I did manage to give up cigarettes and stick to a pipe. The cancer scare worked wonders with my cigarette addiction.

One morning I was talking to Carl Deakin in the village street when old John Hill walked by. Carl Deakin was the owner of the New Fancy colliery which he had inherited from his father. Along with the MacLean father and son who owned the Cannop colliery he was one of the few good colliery owners. When the New Fancy mine was taken over by the National Coal Board Carl Deakin became an Anglican parson, and vicar of Uley on the other side of the river Severn. His son is now Bishop of Tewkesbury.

However, when John Hill walked by he said, "Good marnin'." "Good morning, John," I replied. Carl Deakin was so engrossed in what he was telling me that he did not respond to John Hill's greeting. John walked on a few paces, stopped, turned round and shouted, "Good marnin' to one of yer." John was a great walker. He thought nothing of walking to Hereford and back, a distance of about forty-five miles. Tall and straight he would be seen striding along always carrying his jacket over his arm. If, when there was a cold north wind, one asked him why he was carrying his jacket, he would look surprised and say, "It bain't rainin'." He lived at the Folly on the edge of the village. He was a widower and, much to his regret, childless. "There be the Vicar and his missis, doctor, they've got no children. Them up at Whitemead Park, they've got no children. The Hugheses up at York House, they've got no children. And here be old John Hill, and he's got no children." Then he added, in case I might have come to some wrong conclusion, "Not for the want of trying, mind." When he died the village never seemed quite the same without him.

Minnie the Menace, I used to call her — to myself. There were times when she haunted my surgery. Not for treatment, oh no, but to complain about her neighbours. She lived in a cottage on Berry Hill Meend. They must have had a sticky time of it. I expect they used stronger words than Menace. The disruption with her neighbours would eventually rise to such a crescendo that it became necessary to lure her into Coney Hill hospital until her paranoia had subsided. Then all would be peace again. She would reappear in her cottage some months later, quiet and subdued. But gradually, as time went by, the disruption would be repeated.

She did *once* come into the surgery for treatment. She explained that she had been shopping in Monmouth the day before. As she came out of one of the shops a large dog had knocked her over. I asked her where she had been hurt. She extended a finger on which was a minute scratch. I obligingly put a dressing on it, just to please her. She was very indignant that the dog, a huge creature, she said, had been at large un-attended. She had been to the police station to complain and to demand that the owner should be traced.

A few days later I received a letter from a Monmouth solicitor. He stated that he was acting for a client who had received injuries after being attacked by a savage dog. He named Minnie as his client. He asked me to let him have a medical report, citing the nature and extent of the injuries.

I replied with a letter marked confidential. I described the scratch on her finger, pointing out that I had no evidence as to how it had been caused. I told him, in confidence, that I thought he should know that Minnie had been a patient in a mental hospital on several occasions.

I got a reply to my letter a week or two later. The solicitor informed me that he was no longer acting as Minnie's legal adviser. The police had now traced the owner of the dog. It was the solicitor's dog, a beagle, which had knocked her down, or over which she had stumbled.

Next time Minnie came to the surgery I asked her how her finger was. She replied that it was now alright. She added that the police had found the owner of the dog, who was such a nice man, and had given her a five pound note.

When I drove back from my morning rounds I would sometimes park my car in the forecourt of the New Inn next door to the surgery. There was a wooden bench outside the pub. If the weather was fine I would usually see old Gregory sitting on the bench with his half pint of cider. Occasionally, if I was not too busy, I would go and sit beside him, and treat him to what he called "poor man's champagne", which was a pint of rough cider with a tot of gin added. Usually he would graciously accept a repeat pint.

Gregory was a great character. He had served all through the Boer War, and as a Sergeant-Major had survived the '14-'18 war in France. He was full of stories of his military experiences, most of which needed taking with a large pinch of salt. The stories would get more lurid as the level of the poor man's champagne in his jug fell, especially the level of the second pint. I remember one story he told me. I heard it from him a number of times.

"We had been dug-in in the trenches for a number of weeks, Doctor, and the mud was dreadful. Then we were sent a new company commander. He was one of those temperance chaps, and he stopped the men's rum ration. I had a dreadful time with the men, Doctor. Their moral-y fell so low there was nearly a mutiny. I had to do something about it, so I went along to this new C.O., this pussy footer.

'Sergeant-Major reporting, Sir,' I said.

'What can I do for you, Sergeant-Major?' he said.

'It's about the men's rum ration, Sir, they are missing it, and their moral-y is very low, Sir, very low indeed,' I said.

'Alcohol is very bad for them, Sergeant-Major,' he said.

'Stopping their rum is very bad for their moral-y, Sir,' I said, 'begging your pardon, Sir. I'm having a difficult time with them, Sir.'

'Alcohol is a poison, Sergeant-Major,' he said, 'can you tell me any good it could do for them?'

'Well, Sir, Yes, Sir,' I said 'It's like this. Let me explain. A few days before you took over the command, Sir, I was sitting in my dug-out eating a chunk of bread and drinking my rum ration, Sir. I was sopping pieces of bread in the rum before I popped them in my mouth. A crumb of bread, Sir, soaked in rum, fell on the dug-out floor, and a little mouse came and ate it up. Do you know what happened next, Sir?'

'I have no idea, Sergeant-Major,' the C.O. said.

'Well, Sir,' I said, 'that little mouse picked up a matchstick, Sir, and turned to me, and said, 'Where's that bloody cat?!!' Do you know, Doctor, the men got their rum ration back.''

o   o   o

He was known as Pongo. I often saw him as I drove past the black wooden hut where he lived on the Yorkley to Blakeney road at Yorkley Slade. He was usually sitting on the door-step smoking his pipe, watching the traffic going by. Behind the hut were several steam-rollers. I used to wonder who he was.

Somebody told me his history. He used to live in Lydney, I was told. He was a married man, with several children, holding down a good job — a steady, family man. Then he won a large sum of money on the Calcutta Sweep. I have forgotten how much, but it was six figures. That was years before. As soon as he got the money he abandoned his family, bought the hut at Yorkley Slade, and had been there ever since. He appeared to live from hand to mouth. The only thing he spent money on was buying steam-rollers, which he parked behind the hut. He had hidden his money somewhere.

He was taken ill one day. He asked a passer-by to send for a doctor, as he was in much pain. I went along to see him. The inside of the hut was incredible. It obviously hadn't been cleaned for years. Dirty rags were lying everywhere. Cobwebs festooned everything. There was an old paraffin stove and messy cooking vessels on the floor. His bed clothes were filthy black. So was he. Goodness knows when he had last had a wash or a bath. He had an inflamed gall-bladder. As I bent over him to examine his tummy I realised why he had been nicknamed Pongo. My! how he ponged.

I never learnt his real name. I do not know what became of him. I was never called to see him again. I expect the Public Health authorities moved in. And not before time. But where had he hidden all that money?

It was about ten o'clock one November night when I got a telephone call to go and see Thomas Oliver. He lived up a very narrow lane off the road that leads from Christchurch to Symonds Yat Rock at Readypenny. When I got the message I groaned inwardly. Not only was Thomas Oliver a bit of a cantankerous old man at times, but it was a very foggy night. As I drove nearer to Readypenny the fog became really dense. I had difficulty in finding the narrow lane along which Thomas Oliver lived, by then the visibility was about one yard. Eventually I located it. Carrying my bag in one hand and a torch in the other I groped my way up the lane. The torch was useless and merely threw a white beam a few feet into the darkness. I was beginning to think that I would not be able to find the house, the fog was so thick. Then I saw a faint light shining dimly around the margins of a shut door. "At last," I thought. I found the garden gate eventually by brushing my hand along a hedge until I felt it. I opened the gate and went along a path in the direction of the light shining around the closed door. I arrived at the door and knocked. There was no response. I knocked again, more loudly. After about a minute the door opened at inch and a voice said,

"What d'yer want?"

"I've come to see Mr Oliver," I replied.

" 'Im baint 'ere," said the voice, and the door was closed and I heard a bolt being drawn. After my struggles to get to the house I found this reception more than just disconcerting. I banged loudly on the door. It opened again about an inch.

"I've come to see Mr Oliver," I repeated.

" 'Im baint 'ere, I'm tellin' yer," said the voice and shut the door again, and I could again hear the bolt being drawn. My temper was more than a little frayed by this time. I hammered hard on the door. When it opened, again for about an inch, I said, "If Mr Oliver isn't in, is Mrs Oliver in?" " 'Er baint in," was the reply "nobody baint 'ere but me." "Look here," I said, "I'm the doctor. I've been sent for to see Mr Oliver. I've come all the way in this fog to see him. Why can't I come in? What's going on in this house?" " 'Ouse," said the voice, "this baint 'ouse. 'Ouse be up garden path. This 'ere's the privy."

o o o

Thomas Oliver had spent fifty-five years working at the coal face. He started working down the mines when he was nine years old. He had lived through the unemployment and the depression after World War One and the general strike. He had known difficult times. He had watched his wife and children go hungry. He had been embittered then. His large family had now grown up, providing him with numerous grandchildren.

When the youngest grandchild was a few months old his mother brought him to see me. She was worried about some little white patches that were covering his tongue and the inside of his mouth. I told her it was thrush and gave some treatment for it. A few weeks later the thrush recurred, accompanied this time by diarrhoea. I was acquainted of this by Thomas Oliver over the 'phone, who informed me that " 'e's got ther sparrers again, an' they've gone right through 'im."

It was a sore point with Thomas that he was unable to read or write. It was the only thing about himself that he felt ashamed of. He went to great lengths to hide the fact. He had a sister who had married and settled down with her husband in Swansea many years previously. When she died Thomas went to the funeral. This involved him in a train journey. He wore his best, and only, suit. To boost his ego while travelling he bought a newspaper at the station. He sat in the railway carriage with the other passengers, holding the newspaper in front of his face pretending to read it. Eventually a man sitting opposite to him leant across tapping him on the knee, pointing out that he was holding the newspaper upside down. Thomas glared back at him and growled, "Any bloody fool can read a newspaper the right way up."

One evening Thomas was having a drink in the Rock Inn when a mate of his came in. They started chatting over their cider. His friend mentioned that the previous Thursday he had caught a chub in the river Wye weighing nine and a half pounds. He was a keen angler. Thomas said, "That's funny. I was down fishing in the Wye last Thursday, too, and I fished out a lantern."

"Folks throw a lot of rubbish in the Wye," said his friend.

"But the lantern were alight," said Thomas.

"Doan't tha be a vule," said his mate.

"Well," replied Thomas, "if thou'll knock six pund off tha chub I'll blow out light."

Another evening he was having a drink in the bar of the Speech House after attending a meeting of the Free Miners. An American sergeant with a blonde on his arm was standing at the bar-counter shooting a line in a loud voice for the benefit of the other people in the bar. Thomas was very resentful that American soldiers were stationed in the Forest of Dean during the War. He was very intolerant about the number of half-caste babies being born. One of his daughters-in-law had had one.

He told everyone that he had warned her about smoking cigarettes while carrying the baby. It was coloured brown from nicotine poisoning, he informed everybody.

The Yanks in their high quality uniforms got under his skin. After listening to the American sergeant for some time in the Speech House bar, getting more and more irritated by his loud voice, he could stand it no longer. He got up from his seat. Holding his mug of cider in one hand he walked up to the sergeant. With his other hand he pointed at the American eagle flashed on the shoulder of the sergeant's uniform. The sergeant stopped talking and looked at Thomas. There was a hush in the bar. Then Thomas, still pointing at the eagle, said "That's wrong for a start, mate. It arter be a stork." He then slowly returned to his seat.

Sometimes Thomas would go to the local stores to fetch the groceries if his wife was laid up with her rheumatism. He went to the shop one morning, and flinging the ration books onto the counter said, "I've cum ver rations, an' a doan't want no butter like wot us 'ad last week, neither."

The shopkeeper asked him what was the matter with the butter.

"Matter with un", said Thomas, "matter with 'un. 'Twere turrible. I tasted it an 'twere rancid. The missis tried it, an 'er couldn't get on with it. So us give it ter the dawg. 'E 'ad wun mouthful of it and un tarned right rund an licked 'is arse ter take taste outer'ns mouth."

I once had a disagreement with Thomas Oliver. It concerned a certificate of incapacity for work that I had refused to give to one of his able-bodied sons. Thomas had sent a message asking for a visit. I had made a quite unnecessary journey at a time when I was very busy. Thomas did not agree with my opinion that his son was not incapacitated for work. He disagreed with me in no uncertain terms. I remained firm in my decision not to give a certificate. Much heat was generated.

I cut short the heated argument by walking out of the cottage back to my car, but I inadvertently left my stethoscope behind. Thomas Oliver had the last word of the argument. As I walked down the path back to my car he appeared in the doorway. He shouted after me, "Oi, you. Yer devil. Ye've left yer 'orns behind."

It was during the winter of '47 that I ran into a snow-drift on that short slope leading up to the railway level crossing in Whitecroft. I was on my way to Lydney Hospital. I was well and truly stuck.

35

It was a terrible winter in 1947. The whole Forest was covered with many feet of snow for six weeks or more. Even the road sign-posts were buried. No hedges could be seen. It was a nightmare trying to get about. Most of the places I had to visit were inaccessible by car. Arthur Baynham used to take me round in a large front wheel driven American army lorry. He had bought it very cheaply at a sale of American army surplus stores. There were places where even Arthur Baynham's truck could not get to. Most afternoons I was driven round sitting in a tub which was lashed to a large sledge pulled by a caterpillar tractor belonging to a local farmer. Each morning he visited isolated villages with it, delivering bread and food.

Anyhow, that afternoon I had optimistically attempted to get to Lydney hospital in my own car. It was now axle-deep in a snow drift. A couple of miners from the Princess Royal Colliery on their way home at the end of their shift got behind the car and pushed. Still the car stuck firm, the rear wheels spinning round and burying themselves deeper in the rut as I pressed the accelerator pedal while the miners shoved from behind.

Another miner, a big man with broad shoulders hove in sight. One of the miners shouted to him, "Come on Tottle. Come and give the doctor's car a push." He came slowly towards us. Then he stopped. He looked at the car, he looked at me, he looked at his two mates, then he said, "I will." But as if to justify such an action, he added, "I wouldn't for any other bugger, mind!"

Tottle Morgan had been one of my First Aid enthusiasts. I never learnt how he came to acquire the nickname "Tottle". It seemed to be a very closely guarded secret. I had given some First Aid lectures during the War. When the War was over I did not give any more. First Aiders at that time seemed to belong to one or other of two categories. They either knew the little black St. John's book by heart, had collected a number of medallions for their watch chains, but panicked and were useless at an emergency; or they thought they knew more than they did, tried to take over when anything happened, shouted orders

36

to others, but did the wrong thing themselves. Miss Gould, the Matron of Lydney Hospital, used to say that the little black book should be called not "First Aid to the Injured", but "First Injuries to the Aided". It was said that during the blitz more limbs were lost by the misuse of tourniquets than from the bombs. Today first aid is very different. Tottle belonged to neither of these categories. Tottle was just Tottle. He didn't bother about medallions or passing examinations. He just wanted to be able to help his butties underground, when there was an accident. Although he did his best to hide it, he had a large, warm, compassionate heart.

When the Princess Royal came under the N.C.B. Tottle Morgan was appointed the official in charge of First Aid. He was given a small room from which to operate. He took his new post very seriously, and rightly so. He was invaluable to have about when anything serious happened. He always did the right thing and he knew his limitations. It was a sad day for him when the N.C.B. closed the Princess Royal Colliery and he had to retire.

There were no longer any mates underground to help. So he decided to help them above ground. He stood as a candidate for election to the West Dean Council. Everybody liked Tottle so he romped home at the polls, chosen by his people of White-croft and Pillowell. He now became Councillor Morgan. He next stood for the Gloucestershire County Council. Again he romped home, the choice of his people.

It was not for any personal aggrandisement that he became a Councillor. He was absolutely incorruptible. He just wanted to represent his people, to fight their battles, to see that they were justly treated. In council he brought good earthy common sense into discussions. I don't know what the "Cotswold lot" on the County Council thought of him — the feudal retired army and naval officers, the middle-aged Tory women with double-breasted names, large hats and loud affected voices. To Tottle a spade was as much a bloody shovel in the Cotswolds as it was in the Forest of Dean. He was always courteous, but no respector of persons.

When he grew older he became very verbose, holding up the business of council meetings with long speeches. Any chairman must have found him rather a headache. But nobody would shut him up. He had won so much respect and affection from everybody who knew him that nobody would want to hurt his feelings. In the end it was his health and age that took him from public work.

Tottle Morgan. The last Dobunni chieftain. Chosen by his people. The salt of the earth.

The Forest Hospitals

The Dilke Memorial Hospital, built about a mile out of Cinderford town amongst the trees of the forest, is one of the two Forest of Dean Hospitals. It is known, affectionately, as "The Dilke." I had been shown over it before I settled in the Forest of Dean. One of the factors deciding me to do so was the fact that no surgery was being done there. The Committee was anxious to appoint a surgeon.

A few days after I arrived in Parkend I made a visit to the hospital to discuss with the Matron plans for starting surgery. Her office was opposite the front door. I knocked and was told to enter. It was a cosy room, with a sofa and some comfortable arm chairs. The only sign of an "office" was a small bureau in one corner.

The Matron was elderly. She had on a dark blue dress over which she wore a white coat. On her head was a cap trimmed with lace. On her feet were carpet slippers, the inner sides of each showing large bulges due to bunions. She rose to greet me at the door. As she did so a large chauffeur-driven car drew up at the hospital entrance. Out of it stepped a little old man who was handed a large basket by the chauffeur. The Matron left me at once to greet the old chap. Showing him into her office she rang a bell, and when a maid appeared she ordered tea for three. She introduced me, but I did not catch the name. Who the old boy was I never found out. I never saw him again. He settled himself down in one of the arm chairs, placing the basket at his feet. The Matron made a great fuss of him, chatting away about this and that. I was ignored. Eventually he rose to go. As he did so he said, "I've brought some raspberries for the hospital, Matron. There are eight pounds of them." "Thank you very much," said Matron, "it is very kind of you." "They are sevenpence half penny a pound, Matron. That makes it exactly five shillings."

The Matron went over to the bureau, fetched out a cash-box, extracted a couple of half-crowns which she handed to the old boy, who then asked for his basket back. A maid was rung for to deal with the emptying of the basket, after which the Matron ceremoniously accompanied him back to the car and he was driven off. I then took my leave. I had already spent well over half an hour at the hospital. I had been given much to think about. I saw difficulties ahead of me. That was my first official visit to the Dilke.

When I considered what would be necessary if major surgery was to be performed at the hospital I realised that it was not just a start from scratch that would be needed. Changes would have to be made. I discovered that the hospital did not possess a steriliser. Instruments were being sterilised in a saucepan on an old-fashioned kitchen-range in the hospital kitchen, dressings were put in a biscuit tin and placed in the oven. The operating theatre was quite inadequate. The operating table was a ram-

shackle affair. Only very minor surgery could be done on it.
The hospital corridors were dark and dismal. The two large
wards were dreary places, painted a dark brown, with small
windows letting in very little light.

A large sum of money had recently been raised locally to
build a maternity wing of nine beds. This was near completion
and shortly to be opened. It was a good modern building with a
large delivery room, a sterilising room, a nice nursery, pleasant
light airy wards opening onto a verandah, and a good ward-
kitchen. Once it was functioning the hospital would be a very
lop-sided affair — an inadequate out-of-date main hospital
attached to what would be a modern well-equipped maternity
department.

Another consideration was that it was war time, and although
it was then the early days of the "phoney war" the possibility of
air-raids and perhaps invasion needed to be thought about. The
Infirmary at Gloucester was a very old building, staffed by
physicians and surgeons who, like myself, were also general
practitioners. It was over twenty miles away from some parts
of the Forest. Transport of casualites might be a difficult
problem in an emergency. The Dilke as it then was could only
have dealt with very minor casualties. A lot of money needed
to be raised to modernise the hospital.

The voluntary spirit was very alive in the Forest. It still is,
even after more than a quarter of a century of the National
Health Service. The hospital House Committee and the Ladies'
Linen League that had been responsible for raising the money
to build the new Maternity Wing were more than ready to raise
yet more funds to equip the general side of the hospital. The
biggest problem was to wake up an elderly Matron who regarded
her appointment as semi-retirement. But I must give the old
dear her due, she was really a kindly soul at heart. After putting
up many barriers of resistance she eventually capitulated, on the
condition that it did not involve her in any extra activity. She
handed over all the surgical work to the senior Sister, much to
my relief, as she was a very efficient person.

The hospital had been built a number of years previously for the mining community as a Memorial to Sir Charles Dilke, who had been their Member of Parliament for a long time. It was run by a General Committee, a House Committee, and there was a Ladies' Linen League. It was financed by public subscription, fees from those patients who could afford them, a contributory scheme, and the miners' Sixpenny Fund. Sixpence a week was subtracted from the miners' wages which entitled them and their dependents to free hospital treatment. One representative from each pit collected the sixpences and served on the general committee. It was a thoroughly democratic situation. The Honorary Secretary was a young Chartered Accountant, Mr Geoffrey Barter. He attended the committee meetings and spent an hour or two each week at the hospital in discussions with the Matron. Officials from Gloucester and Bristol are now necessary to do the work he then did. He received no salary for the work. The Medical Staff received no fees, except for the maternity cases, which were paid by the County Council. The House Committee worked very hard under the chairmanship of Lady Betty Crawley-Boevey of Flaxley Abbey.

Flaxley Abbey is a 12th century Cistercian Abbey a few miles from Cinderford. In 1648 it was bought by two wealthy Dutch merchants who were brothers, James and William Boevey. James later gave his share to his widowed half-sister, Joanna Clarke. At her death her son, Abraham, continued in residence. Later, William Boevey, son of one of the original purchasers, married Catherine Riches in 1685 and came to the Abbey to live. When she married William, Catherine Riches was 15 years old. Seven years later she was a widow. She became well known for her beauty, her talents and her charity. Pope, Steele and Addison were her friends. She gave refuge to Bishop Frampton of Gloucester, hiding him in a secret room. She founded the Sunday Schools of England, a work continued in Gloucestershire by Raikes. It was she who promoted the Three Choirs Festival. There is a monument to her memory in

Westminster Abbey. On her death, her cousin, Thomas Crawley, inherited the Abbey. He took the surname of Crawley-Boevey. The Crawley-Boevey family lived in Flaxley Abbey until 1965 when it was sold. Lady Betty and her husband, Sir Lance, left it to live in Spain on account of his poor health. After he died she returned to the Forest of Dean, living at Newnham-on-Severn. She died in 1976.

. Lady Betty followed the tradition of good works set by the famous Catherine two and a half centuries before. Not only was she chairman of the hard-working House Committee but she was also doing her "war work" as a Red Cross nurse, working in the hospital. So she could see for herself what conditions were like, what the problems were, and what needed doing. She was then in her late thirties. She was petite and attractive, full of energy, the epitome of kindliness, had a delightful sense of fun. Everybody was fond of her. As a Red Cross nurse she was not just decorative. She worked hard. No job was too menial or dirty for her to do, whether it was swabbing the theatre floor after an operation or emptying a bed-pan.

As chairman of the House Committee she infused energy into all the members. She set them all onto fund-raising projects. Before very long there was a tidy sum of money to spend. Extra windows were put in the wards to let in more light, and the walls were decorated in cheerful colours. The theatre was equipped with sterilisers, a new operating table, a shadow-less lamp and instruments. Within a year or two the main hospital looked very different.

The other Forest hospital was at Lydney, seven miles from the Dilke. It had an excellent physiotherapy department functioning two mornings each week. It was organised by a Miss Griffin, of Monmouth, a member, I think a founder-member, of the Chartered Society of Physiotherapists. I approached Miss Griffin with a view to her supplying the same facilities at the Dilke. She was very agreeable to this. When I discussed this with the Matron I ran into considerable opposition. She said that the hospital already had a physiotherapist. It turned out that this was a man who came up to the hospital once a week from Cinderford where he practised as a chiropodist. He also had a reputation with local football teams as a bone-setter. She also said that there was no available space for a physiotherapy department. When I mentioned the Boardroom she said it was not suitable. It was a large room, used once a month for Committee meetings. It seemed a waste of space to me.

The Chairman of the General Committee was a Colonel MacLean who at that time was in the Western Desert fighting the Italians. His duties were taken over by the deputy Chairman, a plump elderly man, a buddy of the Matron. One morning I wanted to have a word with the Matron so I enquired of one of the nurses as to her whereabouts and was told she was in the boardroom. So I went along there.

When I opened the door and looked inside there was a revelation in more ways than one. There were the Matron and the deputy chairman sitting side by side; their feet, minus shoes and stockings, were resting on chairs in front of them. The bone-setter, the so-called physiotherapist, was busy as a chiropodist working on four naked feet. There was considerable embarrassment all round. Anyhow, the outcome was that at the next committee meeting it was decided to ask Miss Griffin to start physiotherapy sessions.

Again the House Committee went into action. They soon raised enough funds to buy the necessary equipment. There was soon a flourishing physiotherapy clinic being held on two mornings each week staffed by Miss Griffin and her very competent assistants.*

Some time after this the Matron had a fall, fracturing her hip. It was obvious that she would be off duty for a considerable time. These were days before fractured hips were treated by operation.

*Within a few weeks of the hospital coming under the control of the National Health Service the department was closed down and all the expensive equipment bought with voluntary contributions from the Forest of Dean community was removed to Gloucester Infirmary.

The senior Sister was appointed Acting-Matron. The question of compensation arose, as the Matron was on duty when she had her accident. The Insurance Company asked to see her birth certificate. It took a long time to persuade the Matron to produce it. When eventually she did, it transpired that she was ten years older than everybody had thought, and was about seventy years old. It also transpired that her salary was a mere one hundred pounds a year and that there were no arrangements for a retiring pension. She continued receiving her salary for several years. When eventually Colonel MacLean was de-mobbed and resumed his chairmanship of the hospital he raised a sum of money which was invested to provide a pension for her. It was realised that she would never function as a Matron again. The Senior Sister, who had been Acting-Matron for a number of years, was appointed Matron.

Lydney Hospital was started as a small cottage hospital in 1882 at Aylburton, a village a mile or two outside Lydney, by Mrs Mary Elizabeth Bathurst, the grandmother of the present Viscount Bledisloe. In 1906 it was moved to Lydney. I found that it was a much better equipped hospital than the Dilke. It had nice airy small wards, an outpatient department, a good theatre unit, a casualty theatre, and a Maternity Wing. It was staffed by the local general practitioners, including, when I joined the staff, an old chap in his nineties, still chunnering about "laudable pus." There was also another, Dr. C. O. Carson, a Canadian, who did some good surgery.

The Nursing Staff (and the Medical Staff) were ruled by the Matron, Miss D. J. Gould. And very efficiently indeed did she run the hospital. She had one great pretence — that she was an old battle-axe. Actually she had a heart of gold. She was a nurse of the old school, the Florence Nightingale school, she was a martinet. However her bark was worse than her bite. Grey-haired, bustley, head erect, with her bosom to the fore, she reigned supreme in the hospital. Her word was law.

She had served as an Army Sister in World War One, having been decorated with the Croix de Guerre — "kissed on both cheeks by a French General,'' as she told me a number of times. Her hospital in France had been over-run by the Germans and captured. She and her nurses were put on a train for internment in Germany. When the train had travelled about a quarter of a mile it stopped for a signal. ''Come on girls,'' she said. They all got out and calmly walked back to the British lines.

During World War II her one ambition was to be at the centre of things if Lydney suffered an air-raid. She might even get another decoration. Every time the siren sounded, day or night, she would be on duty, complete with gas-mask, in a couple of minutes or less. Poor Miss Gould, she was disappointed. She didn't get another medal. Lydney never had an air-raid, although from the hospital front steps some nights we could look across the Severn estuary and watch Bristol and Avonmouth getting hell.

Miss Gould made a rule that everybody — she meant everybody — had to keep. Every Wednesday from 10 a.m. until noon everyone in the hospital had to wear a gas-mask slung from their necks. One Wednesday morning I forgot to take my gas-mask with me. Miss Gould promptly ordered me out of the hospital. ''If we had a gas-attack at this moment,'' she said, ''you, who we would be relying on for help, would become a liability.'' So, like a naughty schoolboy, I went away. I did some visits and returned to the hospital after noon to do my rounds.

One morning I went into a ward with her where a young teenage girl was lying in bed sobbing. She had been admitted for an abdominal swelling to be investigated. She had been told that morning that the swelling was a baby. Hence the tears. Such a thing to happen was very much a disgrace in those days. Miss Gould went up to her and stood beside the bedside-locker on which the girl had arrayed various cosmetics. ''Tears won't get rid of it,'' she said.

Then picking up one of the jars of cosmetics from the locker, she read the label and added, ''And rubbing your belly with Pond's Vanishing Cream won't get rid of it, either.''

46

Miss Gould retired in 1945. The new Matron was a Miss Bawden. She did not like the dull-coloured paint used in the hospital. She arranged for the wards and corridors to be painted in light pastel shades. I thought it a great improvement and very attractive. Soon afterwards Miss Gould paid a visit to the hospital to find out if it was still existing without her presence there. She looked at the brightly coloured walls, sniffed, and exclaimed, "Hospital! Hospital! It looks more like an ice-cream parlour than a hospital to me."

The two hospitals, with about eighty beds between them, served the Forest of Dean well. Their appreciation by the community was shown by the financial support they received. They are somewhat more modern today than they were in those days. They did a lot of work, however. About four hundred maternity cases and over five hundred operations were dealt with annually by them.

In 1945 a new X-ray machine was purchased for the Dilke, the money being raised by voluntary subscription. Queen Mary visited the hospital soon afterwards. She showed great interest in it and asked for her hand to be X-rayed. She was shown the wet plate, and the photograph showing the royal bones with Queen Mary's rings is still in existence. Her visit was a great occasion. She inspected the whole hospital, asking very pertinent and searching questions. She held a baby that had been born the previous day. Its mother was the wife of the Vicar of Newnham, now Canon Mansfield. *The Dean Forest Guardian* in its report wrote: "She found little Billy Troutman a very cheery patient." I wonder what became of little Billy Troutman. Crowds of people turned out to greet this much loved royal person. She left the hospital with Lady Betty Crawley-Boevey to have tea at Flaxley Abbey.

That royal visit was a long time ago, over thirty years. Three years afterwards the hospitals were taken over by the National Health Service. Neither Colonel MacLean, the Chairman of the Dilke, nor Lady Crawley-Boevey, was asked to serve on any hospital Committee. The members of the Regional Hospital

Board, the Management Committee and the House Committee were "chosen by the Minister", whatever that may mean. It certainly didn't mean anything very democratic. Today the hospitals are run by the whiz-kids, with marvellous paper qualifications, who know everything about everything except human nature. Ensconced in their offices with fitted carpets, completely remote from patients and the problems at the bedside, they sip their tea.

However, there is now a new large County hospital with genuine medical consultants, a flying squad for maternity emergencies, a blood-transfusion service and a geriatric wing of forty beds at the Dilke. Things almost undreamt of thirty years ago. In spite of a National Health Service the voluntary spirit will not lie down. Through the Leagues of Hospital Friends great improvements have been made with large sums of money raised locally, which would never have been possible from Health Service finances. The hospitals are pleasanter and more human places as a result of their efforts. There isn't much hope for a really efficient Health Service until it is taken out of the murky waters of party politics, or until the politicians recognise that the National Health Service is a responsibility that they must share with those who tend the patients, and are prepared to curb the machinations and self-pampering of an ever growing and remote bureaucracy.

Forest of Dean Coal Mining

"Doctor. I be fair buggered up," Henry Robbins said. He was right. He was. The silica-laden dust he had been breathing for forty years at the coal-face, underground, had seen to that.

He was sitting in an arm chair in a corner of the bar of a small pub. He and his wife lived in the pub with their married daughter who was the licensee. Her husband, Ray Jones, helped out when he was not at work. Ray had a black face. There had been a shot-fire accident some years previously. Powder and coal-dust were embedded in the skin of his face as permanently as if he had been tattooed.

Henry held a court from his arm chair in the corner of the bar, with a little table at his side. On the table were two mugs. One to drink from, the other to spit into. The latter was half-full of black sludgy gelatinous mucus. Every time he breathed, as he expired what air he could, a loud wheeze, high pitched and squeaky, was audible above the conversation in the bar. His face was thin and pinched, the colour grey. His lips were a deep blue, he had not got enough oxygen in his blood to make them red. He enjoyed conversation, but after a few sentences he would have to stop. Talking made him short of breath or started a bout of coughing. I used to feel embarrassed when he coughed, it was so distressing. It shook his whole body, convulsing him, leaving him gasping as he brought up another black globule of sticky mucus. To walk from his armchair to the door of the bar would take him about five minutes. After every few steps he would have to stop to get enough breath to carry on.

"I be fair buggered up," he repeated, "an' they've only given me seventy per cent. compen. 'Owever, it were sixty-five last time." I had heard this sort of complaint before from other silicosis patients. Every now and then I used to get a letter from the Pneumoconiosis Board informing me that on a certain day members of their medical panel would be visiting one of my patients to examine him in order to assess his degree of disability. It was their idea of medical etiquette. Later, I would be told by the patient how he had been assessed. Henry had just been informed that 70 per cent. of his disability was due to silicosis, an Industrial Disease, and 30 per cent. was due to chronic bronchitis. Chronic bronchitis was not an Industrial Disease so he was not entitled to any compensation for thirty per cent. of his disability. So according to the Pneumoconiosis Board Henry was only 70 per cent. disabled. It was a particularly nasty Treasury fiddle. I had written to Mr Philips Price, the Member of Parliament, complaining of the injustice of it. He was sympathetic, but what could one M.P. do against a host of entrenched Treasury officials?

I thought I had better change the conversation to take Henry away from the feeling of being unjustly treated which was rankling in his mind. "Thank your daughter for her letter," I said. "'Ers out shoppin' ", said Henry. I used to arrange my visits before opening time. It was more private. Henry had always been ensconced in his arm-chair long before the bar opened. His wife had had a cyst, about the size of a marble, on her nose. Recently, after a lot of persuasion from her daughter, she had let me remove it at the Dilke. I had just received a letter which read:

Dear Doctor,

I felt I must just write this line to thank you so much for your kindness in attending to mother's nose. It has healed up nicely and we are so pleased it has been removed. She looks much better without it. Thank you very much.

Sincerely yours,

E. Jones.

It was nice to get a letter of thanks occasionally.

Inevitably Henry's condition deteriorated to such an extent that he was no longer able to leave his bed. The bar looked sort of bleak with his armchair empty in the corner. Nobody dreamt of sitting in it although they all knew that Henry would not be occupying it ever again. His heart muscle gave up the unequal struggle of pumping blood to his silicotic solidified lungs. It was failing fast when he asked me, "Tell me, doctor, honest, mind, 'ow much longer 'ave I got?" He was not the sort of chap one could deceive. "About a week, Henry, I should think," I told him. "Ah well," he said looking at me with a grin, "me boozin' and me whorin' days be over."

Joe Willetts lived in an old cottage on a tump in Oldcroft, a hamlet of scattered dwellings off the road from Lydney to Yorkley. Across it ran the Dean Road, built by the Romans, but not much of it is visible now. Joe's family had lived in the cottage for generations. His ancestors had squatted there in the eighteenth century. The Foresters of Dean were the original squatters. They did not squat like today's homeless, in empty houses. In those days they maintained that if a man could enclose a plot of land, build a hearth in it, light a fire in the hearth, and let the smoke arise overnight, he had gained the right to build a dwelling in the enclosure to settle in. It was a widespread practice. By the eighteenth century more than two thousand acres of Crown Land had been encroached on. A "right" was established which the Crown later on had to recognise.

Many of these cottages, still inhabited, exist today, but their number is decreasing rapidly. Some have been modernised. But they are a nightmare to the planners. Today there is a "plan" for the Forest of Dean. It is holy writ, as inviolate as was the Mosaic Law to the ancient Hebrews. Today a dwelling can only be built where the planning experts say it may be built. They do not object to commercial vandalism, the permanent scarring of the Royal Forest of Dean by indiscriminate quarrying, or the horrors of open-cast mining. Of course, the planners themselves do not live in the Forest of Dean. With their inflated salaries they can afford to put their inflated egos into highly desirable residences elsewhere. They do not mix with ordinary work-a-day folk, who don't matter, only the "plan" matters. They appear to me to show an arrogant attitude towards those who provide the cash for their plan they think is a "necessity". In February 1976 Sir Edmund Liggins, President of the Law Society, gave an address to the Royal College of Surgeons. In it he quoted what William Pitt had said in 1783: "Necessity is the plea for every infringement of human freedom. It is the argument of tyrants, the creed of slaves."

Joe Willetts, anyhow, was very happy in his old ancestral cottage. Happy despite the fact that he had been involved in a pit accident several years before. There had been a fall of rock while he was working underground. The rock had fallen on his back, fracturing his lumbar spine and crushing his spinal cord. He was paralysed from the waist down. He was 46 years old. He spent all his time in bed. Wheel chairs were not available then. He was quite interesting to talk to. Having left school when he was twelve years old to go down the pits he was now educating himself. He knew Ruskin, Carlyle, Shakespeare, Dickens and Thackeray.

One day his wife sent me a message asking for a visit. His bladder was giving trouble again. The nerves which supplied his bladder used to be controlled from the spinal cord until it was crushed by that fall of rock.

I left my car on the road at the edge of the grassy tump and started to trudge up the hill to the cottage. I had only gone a few yards when a large gander rushed at me, hissing, with neck extended and its large wings flapping. It was quite frightening. I quickly took my stethoscope out of my pocket and started twirling it rapidly round and round between my legs and the gander's head. That seemed to puzzle him. I hurried as fast as I could up to Tom's cottage twirling my stethoscope all the way accompanied by the irate, hissing, screeching gander. I was very relieved to get into the cottage garden and close the gate between myself and that fearsome bird.

I knocked on the door. Joe's wife answered my knock. "That's a ferocious gander you've got there," I said as she opened the door. 'It's a very fine bird,'' she replied, "had the postman down on Tuesday.''

I can remember when the Princess Royal Colliery at Bream opened the pit-head baths. They were a boon to the fourteen hundred miners who worked there. It was even more of a boon to their wives. No longer would they have the daily chore of filling a zinc tub with hot water, getting it ready by the time their men returned home from their shift.

For those men who lived at Yorkley Slade it was a long tiring trek home from the Princess Royal, uphill most of the way. They would perhaps have already walked a mile or more underground from the coal face to the cage which would lift them to the pit head. They had probably been lying for hours on their sides in a tunnel about two and a half feet high hacking out coal with their picks. Before the pit-head baths were built they would leave the colliery for home in dirty coal-blackened clothes, their helmets on their heads above their black faces, carrying their lamps and their billy-cans. I used to pass them when I was driving around. Many a friendly wave I would get from a man who was quite unidentifiable, looking like a black member of the Black and White Minstrel Show.

There was a bitterly cold north-east wind blowing one January day, before the pithead baths had been installed. A couple of miners left the Princess Royal Colliery to trek back to their homes in Yorkley Slade. The wind cut into them and made them cough. The temptation to call in at the Swan Inn at Phipps Bottom before they tackled the steepest part of their trudge home was too much for them. A good drink of cider in the warm bar out of that Arctic wind was what they could do with. They soon downed a couple of pints each.

They left the Swan and started their walk uphill through Pillowell and Lower Yorkley. They were thinking of that tub of hot water their wives were getting ready for them in front of the kitchen fire. The icy north-east wind blew in their faces making their ears feel like icicles. It was not only their ears that the cold wind affected. After a quart of cider each, it tickled up their kidneys. When they reached Lower Yorkley they realised that they could not last out until they returned home. They went behind a hedge standing side by side, and soon felt very much more comfortable. After one of them had finished he picked up a corner of his coal encrusted dirty old coat and used it as a towel. "Wot be tha a doin' that fer, butty?" his mate asked him. "Eh, last time I went wum with un clean me old wumman 'alf murdered oi," came the reply. Near to where they stood is a hamlet, Yorkley Wood, known to all the local people as *Bunney's Wood*. Surely it must once have been the dwelling place of some Dobunni families; the name, now abreviated to Bunny, having come down the centuries from Celtic times until today.

o o o

Kathleen was eighteen. She was an attractive girl who had been brought up by her aunt. Her father died just before she was born. He had been badly gassed in World War One.

A few years later he developed pneumonia. His damaged lungs could put up no resistance. There were no antibiotics in those days. He died without seeing his baby daughter. Kathleen's mother received no war-widow's pension. The Treasury diddled her out of that. She struggled to bring up her child, denying herself. When Kathleen was five years old she developed pulmonary tuberculosis. Consumption they called it then. It killed her in a few months. She had a married sister, twelve years older than herself who was only too pleased to adopt Kathleen. She had no children of her own. Her husband was a miner. She was a kindly woman. An ardent Baptist, she had been strict in bringing up her niece.

I was very surprised when Kathleen came to see me one surgery and said, "I want you to tell me, doctor, if I am pregnant." I looked at her as she smiled at me. She was not at all upset. I thought of her aunt and what she would say if Kathleen had an illegitimate baby. I should have thought that Kathleen would have been very distraught at the prospect. But no, she sat there quite composed and smiled at me. "When was your last normal period?" I asked her. "Last week," she replied. "Then you are not pregnant," I told her. "But I could be," she said, "you see Tom and I tried last night. We very much want it to happen." "Well," I said, "come back in three or four months time if your periods stop, and I will tell you then." "But I want to know now," she said. "It is impossible to tell you now." "But I want to know now," she said. "It is impossible to tell you today if you only had intercourse yesterday. Was that the first time?" "Oh! yes," she replied. I leant back in my chair and looked at her. "Now, Kathleen, perhaps you will tell me what this is all about," I said to her.

"Well," said Kathleen, "you know Tom?" "Yes," I replied, "I know Tom." I had seen them about together. Tom Barnes was a young miner, a year or two older than Kathleen. He was a decent, steady, straight-forward chap. "Tom and I want to get married," continued Kathleen, "we're very fond of each other; but Auntie won't hear of it. She says I am too

young. So we thought that if I got pregnant she would have to
let us get married. So we tried last night, and now I want to
know if we managed it." I couldn't see any reason myself why
they should not get married if they wanted to. I rather sym-
pathised with Kathleen's bit of blackmail. It was her naivety
I found so surprising. "Come back in three months if you've
had no periods," I told her, "you will just have to be patient
until then."

Kathleen came back in three months. She was pregnant.
There was now the ordeal of breaking the news to Auntie. She,
with Tom, who had been sitting patiently in the waiting room,
went straight away to face Auntie. Auntie couldn't get them
married quickly enough. She had her Baptist friends to think of.
They were a nice young couple, very much in love with each
other. They found a cottage to live in, not much of a place,
but a home, and it was not too near to Auntie. They settled
down to await the baby's arrival. Forty weeks after Kathleen's
visit to the surgery the baby was born. Auntie was thrilled.
She thought it was a most beautiful baby. She didn't seem to
bother very much that her Baptist friends were counting on
their fingers the number of months that had passed since the
white wedding at the Chapel. It is wonderful what the sight of
a baby will do.

Tom was thrilled about his daughter. When he got back
from his shift he would take off his dirty mining clothes, get
into the tub of hot water that Kathleen had got ready for him
and she would scrub his back. When every speck of coal dust
had been removed from his body he got out of the tub and
draped himself in a towel. He then went over to the cot,
gently lifted the baby out, and held her in his arms with a look
of rapture on his face.

It was one of those wretched wet November days, some months
later, when the trees are bare, and the dead leaves lie brown
and sodden on the ground, that my 'phone rang at tea-time.
The manager at one of the local pits was on the other end.
"There's been a roof fall, doctor. We think we'll need you.

Can you come along?'' It really was a depressing sort of day. The rain was a persistent wet drizzle. Patches of mist were hanging about as I drove to the pit. I got out of the car and went to the pit-head. ''They're just bringing him up now, doctor,'' the manager said. I listened to the whine from the engine that was winding up the cage. It stopped at last and the iron doors of the cage clanged open. Four black-faced, grim looking miners, wearing their helmets, carried out a stretcher. They stopped when they saw me. One of them, a deputy, said, ''I don't think there's anything you can do, doctor.'' I stooped down and drew back the blanket. He was quite right. There was nothing I could do.

But there was just one thing I did have to do; one unpleasant thing. It was to go along and tell Kathleen that Tom would not be needing his hot tub that day, or ever again. It was a horrid job. Not the only time I had that sort of job to do.

In 1946 the National Coal Board took over the Forest of Dean colleries. One at a time they closed them all down. The last one to close was the Northern United, on Christmas Day, 1965. The Coal Board decided that the pits were uneconomic. In terms of the economics of human life and happiness the Board was right.

57

Some More Gossip

Miss Payne was an elderly spinster whose brother had been a doctor practising in Coleford years previously. He had never married. Miss Payne had kept house for him. When he first started in practice she drove him round in a pony and trap. Later he bought a motor-car, engaging a chauffeur. It was the first car to be bought by anyone in Coleford. He was a popular and much-loved doctor with an extensive practice. Unfortunately he developed multiple sclerosis. He carried on bravely with his work as long as he could but eventually was forced to retire. He and his sister moved into a large house at Lambsquay. He died a few years before I came to the Forest.

Miss Payne had been bequeathed to me as a patient by my predecessor. She was very fond of dogs. She had five of them, all strays she had adopted, all mongrels. They were of different sizes, and all five were undisciplined. She also kept a goat, which kept straying. She then 'phoned the police to find it for her. She had several nephews. One of them was a doctor, a Medical Officer of Health in another part of the country. He was very attentive to his aunt, visiting her at intervals. He was very solicitous about her health, giving her lots of advice. He was most emphatic that she should have injections of an anti-catarrhal vaccine to prevent her from developing winter colds. Miss Payne was most insistent that I should give her the injections each year. They were quite useless. She still got colds every winter. It was quite a performance giving her the injections. All through the procedure the five dogs were leaping up and down around me and Miss Payne. I had to be very careful that I did not inject one of the dogs by mistake.

Miss Payne had an elderly housekeeper, much older than herself. As time went by it was the housekeeper who was being looked after by Miss Payne. During the war it was extremely difficult to get domestic help. Those two old dears in that large house just could not manage. I gave a certificate to be sent to the Local Labour Exchange stating that on the grounds of age and health they needed domestic help. They sent her a young woman, a refugee.

All went well for a time. Then the peace began to be disturbed each night by an Italian prisoner of war from the camp in Broadwell. He started serenading the refugee outside her bedroom window. How he managed to get out of the prisoner-of-war camp each night I do not know.

The serenading went on for several months. Then about 2 a.m. one night I was telephoned by Miss Payne. She sounded very distressed and in a nearly hysterical state. The refugee was having a miscarriage. I went straight along to Lambsquay. Miss Payne was in a state of extreme agitation, with her hair all awry and without her false teeth. The senile housekeeper was standing about in her nightdress wringing her hands. All five dogs were barking. The pregnant refugee was screaming and shouting in her native tongue, very frightened, with blood trickling down her legs.

I sent for an ambulance and got the miscarrying refugee into hospital. When the ambulance had departed I persuaded the elderly dears to have a hot drink and then get themselves back to bed.

Next morning I thought I had better go along and see how the old ladies were faring after the night of turmoil. Miss Payne had calmed down quite a bit. She was very indignant about what had happened during the night, and what she had been subjected to. "You know, doctor," she said in all seriousness, "the world would be a better place if there were no foreigners in it."

Miss Taylor was a sweet old lady. She belonged to an old Coleford family. One day she showed me one of her hands. Parts of several digits were missing. "That hand was operated on by a burglar," she told me.

She had had a nasty accident to her hand with a lawn mower when she was a young woman. Her doctor had been sent for but was not available as he was away on his summer holiday. The locum tenens he had employed attended instead. I thought he had made quite a good job of her mutilated hand. It was a neat job. Miss Taylor told me she thought he was a very kind and charming man.

He was a professional locum during the summer, working in practices in various parts of the country. The notes he made, however, were not clinical notes. The notes he made were an inventory of the silver and other articles of value in the larger houses he visited. He also made notes about the latches and locks on the doors and windows.

During the winter months he ceased working as a locum. He returned at night to the practices where he had been working during the summer, taking his notes with him. He knew which houses to enter, and how to enter them. He then lifted all the articles of value. He was far away next morning. Nobody suspected the kind doctor who had attended them the previous summer when their own doctor was on holiday. He worked

SOME MORE GOSSIP

this racket for a number of years until he was eventually caught
and did a spell of penal servitude.

I heard a lot of stories from some of my older patients about
one of the previous Parkend doctors, Dr. Maine, who was
something of a character. He wore breeches made of leather
and used to ride around on a motor-bike and side-car. He and
, his wife bred pedigree cats. He had a cat-door in his consulting
room so that the cats could come and go as they pleased. In the
garden I saw several miniature grave-stones with a cat's name on
them.

One day, while he was out on his rounds, somebody left a
message for him. When he returned he picked up the piece of
paper and read the message. On it was written, "Will the
doctor please go to the Speech House Hotel? Lady Dilke's mad."

Dr. Maine leapt onto his motor-bike and roared up Fancy
Hill, turned left at Moseley Green and on to the Speech House.
He parked his motor-bike outside, went in and asked for Sir
Charles Dilke, who was the Member of Parliament for the
Forest of Dean. When he appeared he was asked by this stranger
in leather breeches, "Tell me, Sir Charles, what have you
noticed strange about your wife's behaviour?" The M.P. looked
at him with some astonishment. Then he was asked, "Has she
been violent or been smashing things up?" Sir Charles was then
even more mystified at this stranger asking these questions. As
he did not reply Dr. Maine introduced himself and produced the
piece of paper containing the message and showed it to Sir
Charles. As Sir Charles read it he smiled, and explained to the
doctor that the message should have read, "Will the doctor
please go to the Speech House Hotel? Lady Dilke's maid."

Dr. Maine had long since retired. He was now a very old man.
His wife was completely crippled with rheumatism, and bed-
ridden. They were living at a sea-side resort on the south east
coast. The old doctor looked after his wife himself, doing
everything for her. He had promised her that he would never
let her have to go into hospital to be cared for by strangers.

Marion Smith was a nice young woman. She had just qualified

as a school-teacher. She was engaged to be married to a school-teacher who had enlisted into the army soon after World War Two broke out.

She came to see me the following July. "I'm in trouble, Doctor," she said, "Richard was home on a weekend leave a couple of months ago. I haven't had a period since and I've started being sick each morning. I'm afraid I'm going to have a baby. I don't mind, but I don't know what my mother will say. I just don't know what to do." I knew her mother quite well. She was an ardent church-goer, a pillar of the Mothers' Union, Victorian in outlook. I could well understand Marion's anxiety about how her mother would react when she was told. She would be horrified and very angry.

"Richard is still in this country, isn't he?" I asked her. "Yes," she replied. "Well then," I said, "you let him know at once. Then get married at a Registry Office as soon as you can. Afterwards you can tell your mother you got married on the spur of the moment. The baby will have to be two months premature when it is born. I will try and back you up over that if I can."

Marion took my advice. She slipped up to Catterick and got married to Richard. Mrs Smith was rather cross about the sudden marriage, but she knew these war-time sudden marriages were happening quite a lot with so many young men going abroad. After all, they had already been engaged. She told Marion she had behaved very impulsively. Two months later Marion told her mother she was two months pregnant. Mrs Smith was delighted at the prospect of being a grandmother. It would enhance her standing in the Mothers' Union no end. Richard by this time was in North Africa.

Marion duly went into labour at her appointed time. She had her confinement at the new Dilke Maternity Wing. Everything went off well. As soon as it was over she asked me to telephone her mother at once to tell her that the baby had arrived. Mrs Smith immediately ordered a taxi and came up to the Dilke. She met me in the corridor.

"How is Marion, Doctor?" she asked me.

"Very well," I told her, "just a bit tired."

"And the baby?" she queried.

"A boy," I parried.

"But it is two months premature," she said, "are you sure it is alright?"

"Yes — he's fine," I replied, "there's no need to worry about it."

She then asked the inevitable question, "How heavy is it?" Without so much as batting an eyelid I told her the weight.

"Nine pounds and four ounces."

Mrs Smith gasped. "Thank goodness Marion hasn't got to carry that weight about for another two months," she said.

Mrs Smith was very proud of her two months premature grandson. She told everybody what a fine baby he was. She was, I think, the only person who didn't doubt the prematurity.

Once a month the Ear, Nose and Throat surgeon came to Lydney Hospital from Gloucester to operate on about a dozen tonsil children. The Lydney doctors took it in turn to act as his anaesthetist. They induced them with an ethyl chloride spray and then moved on to open ether. The surgeon was a South African, a crusty bachelor, pompous, and inclined to be bad-tempered. He was not popular with the nursing staff, and with reason. He could be pretty rude to his anaesthetist at times, too. One afternoon he was in a particularly petulant mood. It was Dr. Carson's turn to give the anaesthetics. He was grumbled at about each case. The patient was either too lightly anaesthetised or too deeply. Dr. Carson restrained himself with difficulty.

"I can't remove this child's tonsils when he is as badly anaesthetised as this," the surgeon complained about one case.

Dr. Carson could stand no more. "Well, if you can't, I can," he retorted, and snatching the guillotine out of his hand proceeded to remove the child's tonsils. A tense sort of peace reigned in the theatre for the rest of the afternoon.

He also had tonsil sessions at the Dilke. He was a bit of a

snob and felt rather honoured to have Lady Crawley-Boevey in the theatre. It put him in a more amenable mood. One afternoon, between two cases, he was standing watching her as she was mopping up the blood and mess from the theatre floor ready for the next case. "It is a strange ploy for someone of your station to be mopping up a floor," he said to her. "It's my war-work," she cheerily replied. Then she handed him the mop, saying, "Come on, now, do a bit of war-work yourself. You made the mess, you mop it up." He was a bit taken aback. He handed the mop back to her, and thinking he was cracking a joke, said, "That mop is nearly worn out. I only operate with efficient tools." At the next tonsil session Lady Betty turned up with a brand new mop which she had bought. She had attached a label to it which read, "Mr van der Wet Gibb's mop. Not to be used by anyone else." For the remainder of the war it was an amusing sight to see Mr Gibb and Lady Betty mopping up the theatre floor together after each operation. The theatre sister had great difficulty in keeping her face straight. She was grateful for the mask she wore. When Miss Gould, Matron of Lydney Hospital, heard about it she was green with envy. Wrack her brains as much as she could she could think of no subterfuge which could get Mr Gibb to mop up the theatre floor at her hospital.

Lady Crawley-Boevey developed a sinus infection at one time. It involved her in having to see Mr Gibb in his rooms in Gloucester at regular intervals to have her antrum washed out. It is a rather unpleasant procedure. I commiserated with her when she told me and said I hoped she wasn't being hurt too much. She said she had already had eight washouts and that it was now quite a painless experience. Apparently she had suffered the first time. Instead of complaining she had smiled sweetly at him and asked, "Would you like me to bring you some new-laid eggs the next time I come?" The Crawley-Boeveys ran a farm at Flaxley Abbey. Indeed, her husband, Sir Lance, had a milk-round. Eggs were in short supply during the war, so a dozen new laid eggs were very acceptable. Mr Gibb had his

aged mother living with him. A dozen eggs would be a boon.
"That is exceedingly kind of you, Lady Crawley-Boevey," he
replied. At her next visit she turned up with a basket containing a dozen new laid eggs. "I've brought you the eggs,"
she said as she arrived. "Thank you very much indeed, Lady
Crawley-Boevey," replied Mr Gibb. She then took out the
eggs one at a time and laid them in a row on his desk. "Every
time you hurt me I'm putting an egg back in the basket," she
said. After her antrum had been washed out there were only
four eggs left on the desk. At her next visit there were seven.
Every time after that Mr Gibb had a dozen eggs to take home
for his aged mum.

The monks from the Cistercian Abbey at Flaxley felled trees
in the forest during the thirteenth century. They sold the wood
to be burnt for charcoal, which was used to smelt the iron-ore
that was being mined. The monks were greedy. They felled
the trees indiscriminately. Eventually the king, Henry the
Second, had to restrict their activities. He granted them a
patch of forest of about 900 acres for their use, prohibiting
them from felling trees anywhere else in the forest. He also
restricted them so that they were allowed to cut down only one
oak tree each week in their enclosure. It was called, and still is,
Abbot's Wood. Later somebody built a large house there,
called Abbotswood House, about a mile away from the Dilke.
In the 1930's and '40's it was occupied by a Roman Catholic
Order of Nuns, the Blue Sisters. They were state registered
nurses running a nursing home. It was a very good nursing
home, with a very high standard of nursing. They also had a
farm, using the produce in the home. The Mother Superior,
a well educated Irish woman, had been in charge of the physiotherapy department at St. Thomas's Hospital before taking her
vows. She possessed a dry sense of humour.

I attended a number of patients at Abbotswood nursing home.
I got to know the Blue Sisters, who were a cheerful, un-
sanctimonious group of women. They were excellent nurses.
Unfortunately the home later had to close down for economic

reasons. Their fees were too low and the running costs too high.

Sister Marie, a French-Canadian nun, had been a member of the Order for many years. She was a short, round, chubby, cheerful woman. She had to be admitted to the Dilke for a major abdominal operation. She was nursed in a single room. Because of the shortage of nurses at the Dilke at that time the Mother Superior sent along one of the Blue Sisters to nurse her.

I popped into her room as she was coming round from the anaesthetic. Sister Marie was swearing like a trooper and jabbering some French words I didn't understand. The little Blue Sister who was standing by her bed looked very embarrassed when she saw me. She shook Sister Marie by the shoulder gently, and said, "Hush! Hush Sister, or I shall have to tell the Reverend Mother."

"To hell with the Reverend Mother," responded Sister Marie.

"It's alright, Sister," I said, "she doesn't know what she is saying. You've seen patients coming round from an anaesthetic before."

"But such dreadful words," said the little Blue Sister.

"Don't take any notice of it," I told her, "the sedative will soon be taking effect. Then she will sleep. When she wakes up she won't know anything of this. Please don't tell her. We both know Sister Marie, she would be very upset if she knew. Nobody need know but you and me."

Next morning when I visited her, Sister Marie was lying propped up in her bed with a lace shawl over her head. Her eyes were closed. She was counting the beads on a rosary. As she counted, her lips moved. The little Blue Sister glanced my way. She gave me a sort of knowing-look, quite demurely. I gave her back a sort of knowing-look, quite demurely. Sister Marie continued counting her beads, her lips moving, her eyes closed.

It is the one and only time I've shared a secret with a nun.

One of the patients I attended at Abbotswood nursing home

was a small boy with severe asthma and bronchitis. He lived
with his parents in a rather strange community, a sort of religious
commune. It consisted of several married couples and their
children who all lived together in an old large farmhouse,
sharing everything. They told me that they were searching for
eternal truth, or something like that, by all living cheek-by-
jowl with each other. Anyhow, it was an experiment that did
not last very long. One member was a potter, another did
horticulture, another did carpentry. The women shared the
cleaning and the cooking and fed the hens. The father of my
little patient did the praying, spending hours in prayer, and
meditation. He was regarded as a sort of saint. I'm not sure
whether his wife thought he was a saint. I certainly thought
there was a relationship between his saintliness and his son's
asthma attacks. When he was not absorbed in prayer and
meditation he was a terribly fussy individual. He was very
fussy over his child, especially when he had an attack of asthma,
which was often. It was not sufficient for me just to attend the
child when he had an attack. It involved me in long telephone
conversations about the child. He invariably rang me up when
Tommy Handley was broadcasting. That did not help. One
attack of asthma was particularly severe. The more the father
fussed the worse the asthma became. So I persuaded the parents
to let me admit him into Abbotswood nursing home. It was as
much to get the child away from his father as anything. But he
kept visiting the boy. He was an awful nuisance to the Blue
Sisters, demanding this and that, criticising this and that, and
interfering. It was marvellous how patient those nuns were
with him.

The Mother Superior came with me to the front door as I was
leaving one day. I was feeling rather guilty about involving them
all with this case. "I hope, Reverend Mother," I said to her,
"that the boy's father is not being too much of a nuisance to
the Sisters." "No. No," she replied. Then added, "They tell
me he is supposed to be a saint." There was a silent pause as
we stood on the top front-door step. Then she said, in a rich

Irish brogue, "I think it is possible that the blessed Saints in Heaven must sometimes try the patience of the Almighty almost beyond endurance."

The Forest of Dean at War

It was a beautiful summer evening in 1940, with glorious sunshine and a cloudless blue sky. I went into the waiting room just before evening surgery to dump some magazines for the patients to read. The outside door was wide open. Two early patients were standing on the doorstep in the sunshine. A squadron of Spitfires flew overhead. The two Foresters stared up at them. I heard one of them remark; "Eh! I wouldn't like to be up there in one of them things." The other replied, "I wouldn't like to be up there and *not* in one of them things."

The "phoney way" was over. France had fallen. The Dunkirk evacuation had been completed. Britain stood poised to withstand invasion. It all seems so unreal now, looking back on it thirty-seven years later — Churchill's famous rallying call to the nation to resist, the spontaneous formations of the Local Defence Volunteers, Lord Haw-Haw, the removal of all road signs, the rumours of spies being dropped by parachute, the evacuees with their gas-masks slung from their necks.

My telephone rang later that night. P.C. Fardon was on the other end, ringing from the police station at Yorkley. "Can you come along, Doctor?" he said, "one of my specials has been shot." I drove up to Yorkley. Outside the Co-op shop on Bailey Hill a black saloon car with its masked headlights on had swerved across the road, blocking it. The tall, very plump, constable was standing beside a body lying slumped on the pavement. It was a fairly dark night. I could dimly see a few other figures about with arm-bands, on which were printed the letters L.D.V. One of them held a rifle, the others held pikes. Where they got the pikes from I never learnt. What use they would have been against Panzer tanks I couldn't understand. I dropped onto one knee and flashed my torch on the man lying on the pavement. He was very dead.

"Who is he?" I asked P.C. Fardon. "He's one of my specials," he replied, "he's just gone off duty. He was on his way home in his car. He lives in Drybrook." "What happened?" I asked. "This chap shot him," replied the constable. He went over to the man with the rifle, took it from him, and said "I'll take charge of that." "He should have stopped when I flashed my torch," said the man. I recognised him. He was an elderly man who lived in Oldcroft. He had been in the Boer War and the '14 to '18 war, an old soldier. He was holding a torch in his hand. It was about the size of a packet of twenty cigarettes, and had a piece of red paper fixed over the bulb by a rubber band. "He should have stopped," he repeated. "We'll see what the Coroner has to say about that," P.C. Fardon told him. He was angry and upset. "He's put himself in charge of the L.D.V.," he said to me.

The next night I had another call to Yorkley. This time to see a sick child. I drove carefully, keeping a keen look out for any tiny red lights being flashed. On the way back, as I got to the railway level-crossing at Parkend, a hurricane lamp with a red cloth over it was being waved in the middle of the road. I stopped at once. Some figures came towards me. I wound down the car window. "What's up?" I asked. A bayonet was suddenly thrust through the open window in front of me, and a light flashed on my face. Then a voice said, "Oh! It's only the doctor," and the bayonet was withdrawn. The L.D.V. were on duty again. As I undressed before going to bed that night I noticed that the knot in my tie had been cut by the bayonet. I suddenly went all hot and cold as I realised how near that knot was to my carotid artery. Next morning I telephoned the Coroner. I thought that he should know about this near-miss before he held his enquiry on the other incident which had not been a near-miss.

The Coroner, Mr M. F. Carter of Newnham, was a grand old chap, a terrific walker. He walked from his home in Newnham to where he was holding his inquests holding a long staff in his hand as long as himself. At the enquiry about the special constable's death the old soldier tried to justify himself. "I saw this car coming," he said, "I flashed my torch. The car did not stop, so I fired." The Coroner did not mince his words. He ordered the police to stop the carrying of unauthorised arms and sent a report to the War Office.

The Local Defence Volunteers were disbanded soon after this and the Home Guard was formed. At any rate in the Forest of Dean the Home Guard was no "Dad's Army". It was an efficient, disciplined, well armed body of men — tough miners. If ever the Nazis had invaded Britain and reached as far as the Forest of Dean they would have found waiting for them guerrilla bands every bit as efficient as Tito's partisans. They would have resisted, as their ancestors did the Romans and the Angles. I know. I was their M.O. But until the Home Guard was formed things were pretty comic as well as tragic. One group of L.D.V.'s stopped a hearse containing a coffin and demanded to look inside, only to find the corpse of an old fellow who had died in Westbury Infirmary. Another group marched a visiting clergyman to Lydney Police Station with a gun in his back. They informed the station sergeant that "they're comin' down in 'Olland dressed like this." Everybody knew somebody who had heard Lord Haw-Haw state on the wireless that the Germans knew that Blakeney Church clock was ten minutes slow.

Many evacuated families arrived from Eastbourne. I had always imagined Eastbourne to be a posh sort of place. The condition of most of the evacuees from there revealed that a great deal of poverty existed in the town. All were found homes and were welcomed. The compulsory powers that existed did not need to be used in the Forest. There had already been evacuees from London. One woman who had arrived with her children from the East End told me that she had had to leave her elderly mother behind. She had told her daughter that she wasn't going to be turned out by that Hitler or anyone else. Soon after the air raids on London started the woman came to see me. "My old mum has had it," she told me, "the house got a direct hit. I don't think she suffered at all. It was quite a sudden end. Anyhow, they couldn't find 'er 'ead anywhere."

I was also M.O. to a Prisoner of War Camp at Broadwell. There I had the help of two good medical orderlies. There were German and Italian prisoners in the camp. After the war had ended a number did not wish to be re-patriated. They settled down in the Forest, marrying local girls. They were accepted by the community without any recriminations or ill-feeling.

The 131 Forestry company of the R.E.'s were stationed in the Forest, not leaving until well after the Normandy landings. They were a grand lot of fellows. They were commanded by a Major Clarke, an excellent officer, much respected by his men. I found him to be a delightful person and got to know him and his wife quite well. I was M.O. to the Company, as there were not enough personnel to justify the employment of a full time Army M.O. The day after the Germans capitulated Major Clarke trod on a mine in a forest in France and was killed.

The Nazis did not invade the Forest of Dean but the Yanks did. They were not popular. We had white Americans and

Negroes. It was the former who were unpopular. They took over the Forestry School in Parkend as their headquarters. A British officer, Major Mitchell, was posted as Liaison Officer between the Americans and the civilian population. He was kept busy. He was a pleasant, tactful Scot. He needed all his tact.

One morning I had an appointment to see Major Mitchell who had his office in the American headquarters. As I went into the Forestry School my way was blocked by a rifle held in front of me. A tall Negro soldier said, "You no can come in," I told him I had an appointment to see Major Mitchell. "You no can come in," he repeated. I took the Major's letter out of my pocket and showed it to him. "You no can come in," he said yet again. Then he added, "Try the back door, sor, there's no guard there."

I went in by the back door and was directed to a large room where there were several trestle tables loaded with papers. Major Mitchell was sitting behind one. American officers sat at the others. While I was talking to the Major a white G.I. came in, hands in trouser-pockets, his head uncovered, and a cigarette dangling from his lips. Still with his hands in his pockets he stood in front of the trestle next to Major Mitchell's. The American officer told him that what he had typed was not satisfactory and he must type another copy. "If I can get round to it," said the G.I. and sauntered off, still with the cigarette dangling from his mouth. The American officer turned towards Major Mitchell, gave his shoulders a shrug, and said, "What can one do?" "Clap him in irons!" Major Mitchell bellowed back. For once his tact had deserted him.

The Americans who were stationed in the Forest of Dean were, I should think, the equivalent of our Pioneer Corps. Their main job was stacking poison gas in the Forest. They stacked hundreds of thousands of tons of it. It took several years to remove it all when the war was over. It was, of course, never used. I often felt very apprehensive about the possibility of those stores of gas being bombed. Some bombs fell in the

Forest, but luckily none of them hit any of the stores of poison
gas. Incendiary bombs were another hazard. Look-out points
were erected by the Forestry Commission, being manned day
and night.

The Americans were the worst and wildest drivers of lorries
I have ever encountered. There were a number of fatal accidents,
mainly of children being run over. At every inquest the driver
of the lorry was not available to give evidence. He had been
flown out of the country by the authorities immediately after
the accident. The Coroner was very angry and frustrated about
it, but he was unable to stop the practice.

About 1 a.m. one morning I was called out by the police
after a road accident on one of the two sharp bends at the top of
Speech House hill. A jeep, with four American officers in it,
had overturned. Two were unconscious, one had a badly
fractured pelvis, the fourth had a fractured femur. I had them
admitted to the Dilke pending their transfer to an American
Army hospital. I telephoned the American headquarters
asking them to inform their M.O. He turned up about 7 a.m.
He arrived at the hospital a bit bleary-eyed, was taken to the
ward where the four patients were, gave them a cursory glance
and asked if we had a telephone. He said he must ring the
General. Eventually he got through. "Hullo! Is that you
Gen.?" he asked. He then told the General what had happened
and asked for instructions. He listened to the General's instructions, and then said, "O.K. Gen." and replaced the
receiver. Eventually an American ambulance arrived and he
departed with the four patients. I had lost a night's sleep. He
did not even thank me for what I had done. His attitude seemed
to be that I was personally responsible, not only for the accident,
but seemingly, for dragging him away from a girl-friend.

During the weeks before D-day the Americans were very
busy stacking 1,000 lb. bombs along the grass verges on the
sides of the roads — hundreds of them. Then one day there
was terrific activity as they were rapidly collected, put on
lorries, and whisked away. We knew then that the invasion of

74

the continent was imminent. The Americans themselves departed with the bombs, leaving somebody else to shift all that poison gas they had left behind. The negro soldiers were sadly missed by the Forestry Commission. They had kept down the grey squirrel population. They used to catch them, skin them, stick a piece of wood through them, roast them on an open fire, and eat them. Everybody else rejoiced at the end of the American occupation.

They were strange, busy, years during the war. Driving about at night with masked headlights, especially in fog, was a hazard, made worse by the wandering over the roads of the forest sheep. Overhead was the route taken by the German bombers on their way to Birmingham and Coventry, and the towns and cities of the Midlands and Merseyside. The drone of their engines as they flew overhead became a familiar sound. On their return journey if they had any bombs left they would drop them on any light they saw. This happened every now and then in the Forest, once in Parkend.

The miners were told not to go to work with their lighted lamps at night as was their custom. They, of course, ignored the rule. One evening I suddenly heard the rat-tat-tat of machine-gun fire. It turned out that a group of miners on their way from Parkend to Cannop Colliery were carrying their lighted lamps as usual. A German plane had nose-dived and machine-gunned them. By a miracle nobody was hit. But I never saw a lighted lamp being carried by a miner again until the war was over.

One German plane crashed at Coalway. Mrs Voisey, who was doing her war-service as a woman special constable, driving a police car, saw the two pilots parachute down into Nagshead Wood. She went along in the car and picked them up. I met her as she was driving them to Parkend Police Station. She stopped and spoke to me from the car. "I've just picked these two up," she said, nodding her head to the back seat where two grey-uniformed figures sat hunched up, "they are not injured. But to think that I was nervous about arresting them! Look at them! They are both only sixteen years old." This happened during that stage of the war when Goering was running short of pilots for his Luftwaffe and was using schoolboys.

One afternoon there was an air-raid on Gloucester. A munitions factory was bombed. A number of people from the Forest of Dean were employed in the factory. The bombing occurred at the end of a shift, just as the workers were leaving the factory. There were several deaths. One man who lived in Parkend was knocked out by the blast. He came to a few hours later to find himself locked in the mortuary with a number of corpses. He was in a "bit of a state" when he got back home. Some people thought it was funny, but it had not happened to them.

Albert Jones was a young chap who had joined the army at the outbreak of the war. He had been posted to the north-east corner of India where he had contracted the tropical condition, sprue. He had been discharged from the army on medical grounds. Sprue is a condition affecting the absorption of fats from the intestine. A high protein, no-fat, diet is essential during treatment, and for a long time afterwards. He came to see me the day after he returned home. He was very thin, pale, and looked far from well. He needed assistance with his special diet. The Ministry of Food, under Lord Woolton, the Food Minister, had issued a regulation enabling sufferers from sprue to obtain extra meat and other rations in exchange for their butter ration, and also dehydrated bananas. While in the military hospital Albert had been fed on a large number of bananas as a part of his treatment. He was convinced that they were essential. Dehydrated, or any other sort of bananas were not available to the general public during the war. Albert asked me for a certificate to take to the local Food Office stating that he suffered from sprue. I gave him one. He came to see me the next day to tell me that the Food Office had accepted my certificate and he had been given the special rations. But they told him that if he needed dehydrated bananas his doctor must send them a report on the fat analysis of his stools. Albert was very upset at not getting his bananas. I telephoned the Food

Office asking why my certificate was valid for all the other articles of diet but not for the dehydrated bananas. I was told firmly, "No fat analysis, — no dehydrated bananas." I pointed out that I had not the facilities to carry out the analysis, that even if I had, I was too busy as there was a war on. I was again told, "No fat analysis — no bananas."

' So I wrote a letter to the Ministry of Food saying that if they wanted the analysis to be done they must do it themselves. I also told them that to make it possible for them to do it I was sending a jam-jar of Albert Jones's stools to Lord Woolton's private residence, pointing out that if Lord Woolton took no action I was quite sure that Lady Woolton would. I thought that would knock a bit of common sense into officialdom. Not a bit of it. They took the letter seriously. I was telephoned from three different departments of the Ministry of Food from three different parts of the country beseeching me to postpone the despatch of the jam-jar. Albert got his dehydrated bananas.

Mary Sims came to see me one day. She was a single woman in her mid-thirties employed as a secretary-typist in the local Council Office. She was very anaemic and in a nervous state. She said that her work was getting her down and that she was overworked. Wartime regulations added a lot of work for local authorities. She obviously needed a rest for a week or two while her anaemia was being treated. I gave her the usual Health certificate. She came again the next day saying that her boss also wanted a certificate. So I gave her one which stated that she was incapacitated on medical grounds. She came again the following day, bringing the certificate back, saying that her boss insisted on a diagnosis on the certificate. This was too much for my patience. Anyhow, her medical condition was her private affair and of no concern of her employer. He rejoiced in the Christian name of Hector. So I wrote on the certificate that she was suffering from "Hectoritis" — which was partially true anyhow. Hector, like Queen Victoria, was not amused. He brought the matter up at the next Council Meeting. After a long and serious discussion the Council decided that there really was not anything they could do about it. Not even laugh.

The Bugler
of the Old Contemptibles

It does not take very long to travel to India or back nowadays. Thirty and more years ago there were no airways. It was a three week voyage by P. & O. or the old City Line. There was plenty of time to sit around on the deck and read. During my return to England after being away from it for some years I began to think about my own country again. I had with me on the voyage a book of Masefield's Collected Poems, it being a favourite of mine. All the time I was in India it had remained unopened. Packing up to return home I had put it aside to read during the voyage. Masefield lived in and wrote about a part of England I knew well, the Herefordshire-Worcestershire border country with the Malvern Hills linking the two counties. I was looking forward to seeing it again. I was sitting on deck reading it one day when a fellow traveller next to me said "I see you are reading Masefield's poetry." "Yes," I replied, "He writes about a part of England I am particularly fond of." He asked me if I knew of a collection of poems entitled "Gloucestershire", by a poet named F. W. Harvey. When he discovered that I did not know it he insisted on lending me a copy then and there. In the mood I was in, thinking of my return to England, I read them with delight. Here was no airy-fairy stuff. Like Masefield he wrote about the countryside and about people, real people. The poems were alive and vivid. When I arrived back home I purchased a copy.

A few weeks after settling in the Forest of Dean a patient came to see me during one morning surgery. He was a middle-aged man, short, bespectacled, dark haired, and with a slight stoop. He seemed a bit shy, speaking with a soft gentle voice. On asking him his name he replied, "F. W. Harvey." "I have been reading a book of poems by someone of that name," I said. He gave a smile, confessing that he was the author. Thus started an acquaintanceship which lasted until his death seventeen years later. From the memory of that relationship, from what I have learnt about him from other people, and from what I have discovered from reading his poems, I am now able, to a certain extent, to reflect on and recollect the personality of this Gloucestershire man.

F. W. Harvey was essentially a patriot and a country lover. He had a nature that combined a love of out-of-doors with an ability to play cricket, football and hockey exceptionally well. He was a great cricketer, playing for Gloucestershire on several occasions. With all this physical activity he also combined a love for the Arts, for poetry and music. He loved music and had a good voice as a singer, and encouraged folk-music in the district — the choirs, and the silver and brass bands. Across the fullness, the enjoyment and the happiness of his life as a young man fell the shadow of approaching war: the threat from German militarism to the freedom and safety of England, a threat to all he held so dear. He realised that he might soon be called upon to fight to protect these things and perhaps to give his life. He looked for a faith to make such a sacrifice worthwhile. He found in the life of Jesus of Galilee and in the tenets of the Roman Catholic Church the plain meaning of sacrifice. In this and in the defence of his homeland he discovered a faith and a cause. All this found expression later in his poetry.

In 1914 when England went to war with Germany Harvey immediately volunteered for active service. He enlisted in the 5th Battalion of the Gloucestershire Regiment. His comrades were the men and lads of Gloucestershire. He soon found himself alongside them in the trenches of France and Flanders. He joined as a private soldier, soon becoming a corporal. Later he was given a commission. In the trenches the battalion produced a newspaper, the Fifth Gloucester Gazette. Harvey contributed many early poems to it. They were collected together with some pre-war poems and published in book form in England in 1916 with the title "A Gloucestershire Lad at Home and Abroad." The poems were written during lulls between the battles. When there was action he was anything but the "dreamy little man" he described himself as in a self-portrait poem. In August 1915 he was decorated for "conspicuous gallantry." In 1916 while on individual patrol as a scout inside the German trenches he was taken prisoner. He found himself in a prisoner-of-war camp in Westphalia together with a thousand other prisoners of various nationalities. It was a traumatic experience for him. Penned up behind barbed-wire, useless to his country, lonely for home, remembering his comrades still fighting in the trenches, frustrated by having all his vitality suppressed, it was almost more than he could bear. He poured out his feelings in verse. Writing poetry was one means of escape. He did escape physically from the camp one day hidden in a basket. He was recaptured but again escaped by jumping through the window of a moving train bringing him back to captivity. The poems he wrote while a prisoner he sent home to his mother. German censorship made no objection to them. They were published in a volume entitled "Gloucestershire Friends" while he was still in the prisoner of war camp. One day, while lying in his bunk he noticed that a fellow prisoner had chalked on the wall opposite to him a sketch of a reedy village pond with ducks swimming on it. Harvey got out paper and pencil and wrote what is his best known poem — "Ducks." It starts:

"From troubles of the world
I turn to ducks,
Beautiful comical things"

and concludes

"When God had finished the stars and whirl of coloured suns
He turned his mind from big things to fashion little ones;
Beautiful tiny things (like daisies) He made, and then
He made the comical ones in case the minds of men
Should stiffen and become
Dull, humourless and glum,
And so forgetful of their Maker be
As to take even themselves — quite seriously.
Caterpillars and cats are lively and excellent puns:
All God's jokes are good — even the practical ones!
And as for the duck, I think God must have smiled a bit
Seeing those bright eyes blink on the day He fashioned it.
And He's probably laughing still at the sound that came out of
its bill!"

At last came the armistice of November 11th, 1918. But it was not until the Easter of 1919 that Harvey returned home again. The joy of the homecoming was overshadowed by the death of his brother, Captain E. Harvey, M.C. and bar, of his own regiment, killed in action within one week of the end of the war. His father and another brother had died earlier. Many of his friends had been killed. Nevertheless, all the frustrated energy pent up inside him during three years of captivity was suddenly released. He married, settled in Yorkley in the Forest of Dean practicing as a Solicitor. He continued with his poetry. Writing poems about nature and the countryside, poems about animals, about people, about children, and about England and home, some of them in Gloucestershire dialect. Much of it is folk poetry. Through all the poems runs his religious faith, giving them a mystical quality.

One of the happy events which he helped to institute was the great annual festival of music when hundreds of people would gather on Whit-Sunday afternoon among the fresh green beech-trees, the oaks and the bluebells in the Devil's Chapel to listen to the singing of the Whitecroft Male-voice choir. The Devil's Chapel consists of ancient iron-mines dating from Roman (perhaps pre-Roman) times, situated between Bream and Lydney. Huge grotesquely shaped iron-limestone rocks covered with moss by the passage of time, some of them split by the roots of ancient yew trees, alternate with deep caverns from which the iron-ore had been extracted two thousand years ago. It is a place of magic and enchantment.

F. W. Harvey longed to awaken ordinary folk to beauty, bringing out their hidden talents. He expresses this longing of his in the poem, "The Bugler," written long before:

"God dreamed a man;
Then, having firmly shut
Life like a precious metal in his fist,
Withdrew, His labour done. Thus did begin
Our various divinity and sin.
For some to ploughshares did the metal twist,
And others — dreaming empires — straightway cut
Crowns for their aching foreheads. Others beat
Long nails and heavy hammers for the feet
Of their forgotten Lord. (Who dares to boast
That he is guiltless?) Others coined it: most
Did with it — simply nothing. (Here, again,
Who cries his innocence?) Yet doth remain
Metal unmarred, to each man more or less,

Whereof to fashion perfect loveliness.
For me, I do but bear within my hand
(For sake of Him our Lord, now long forsaken)
A simple bulge such as may awaken
With one high morning note a drowsing man:
That wheresoe'er within my motherland
The sound may come, 'twill echo far and wide
Like pipes of battle calling up a clan,
Trumpeting men through beauty to God's side.''

After the war came the black days of the twenties, with mass
unemployment and the general strike. There was severe
suffering and poverty in the Forest of Dean. People came to
Harvey with their troubles and problems. He represented them
in the Courts when necessary, even though his clients were
sometimes unable to pay him his fees. His eloquence in Court,
a number of people have told me, would sometimes bring tears
into the eyes of the Magistrates, as he related to them the
background of the poverty and distress. Harvey shared his
clients' poverty, sometimes he was desperately poor. However,
he was not just a lawyer. He was also a poet. He hoped that
such events as the festival in the Devil's Chapel, the joys of
music and art, would act as a balm to their sufferings. Money
and social status were not high in his scale of priorities. He was
blest that his wife shared his attitude and his ideals. She sus-
tained him in all his efforts. His needs were simple and un-
complicated. He never owned a car. His books, his memories,
and his religion were his solace. All this found expression in his
poetry.

Gradually, during the thirties, he became disillusioned. His
years in the prisoners of war camp had inflicted psychic trauma
from which he never really recovered. He had been permanently
scarred. He was a war casualty although he would have been the
last to have admitted it. He was elbowed out of the music
festivals at the Devil's Chapel by self-important local worthies
who fancied themselves as politicians, tiny village Titos. He

became rejected, together with what he stood for. He began to feel the cynicism and disaffection in literature, in music, and in art that matched the political betrayal of principles for which the citizen-soldiers of the first world war had fought, believed in, and died for. The dream of "The England to be," born during the war, did not materialise. The little junta of petty local politicians, full of their self-importance, parochially minded, jealous of the power they could wield by the spending of other people's money had no use for Harvey's genius. Some of them had pleasanter, more genuine personalities than others. Some had not read what St. Paul wrote to the Christians in Galatia who were Celts, translated in the Jerusalem Bible, as: "it is the people who are not important who often make the mistake of thinking that they are." Harvey increasingly found his companionship in village pubs amongst ordinary humble men. All that abounding vitality that had been his was beginning to ebb away. He had never been interested in money. He never thought a day ill spent if he had lived it among friends new or old. Strangers enjoyed meeting him in the pubs when they were on holiday, finding that he added a new dimension to their lives by his company, his manner, and his charm. Yet all that abounding energy that had been his was beginning to dry up.

Then the Second World War loomed on the horizon, with the Nazis beating the battle-drums and striding arrogantly across Europe. The prospect of the agony of another war, the memory of his many comrades who had lost their lives in the last one, believing, as they had been told, that they were fighting a war to end all wars, added to his disillusionment. It was at this stage in his life that he walked into my surgery that morning and I met him for the first time. At first I only saw him very occasionally, but later on his visits became more frequent. He was then building a shell around himself. It was a whelk-shell, so it had an opening. He kept it closed with a curtain of shyness. As I saw more of him he would raise the curtain enabling me to discover something of the man inside the shell.

In spite of his disillusionment, his spiritual injuries and his suffering he never became bitter or cynical, there was no self-pity. That is a great triumph of the spirit.

The musical festival in the Devil's Chapel was able to survive the war for only a year or two. With the death of the conductor of the choir it never again revived. After the war, when life became so brash, it was forgotten. It was, perhaps, inevitable that Harvey's frequent visits to the local pubs earned him the reputation of being a drinker. He made no apology for this in his poem "Apologia". All I can say is that I never once saw him the worse for drink. What is impressed on my memory of him is his gentleness. He took a simple unaffected pleasure on discovering that I knew and enjoyed the poems in his book "Gloucestershire". One day he left a book at my house with a note saying it was for me. It was another collection of some more of his poems, then, as now, out of print, entitled "A Gloucestershire Lad". It was dedicated "To All Comrades of mine who lie dead in foreign fields for love of England, or who live to prosecute the war for another England."

During the last ten years or so of his life his health gradually failed. Added to this were money problems. He had never been very interested in making money, especially out of other people's misfortunes. He conducted legal affairs almost to the end of his life. At the end, on my daily visits to him a smile always lit up his face although he was very weak. He could even then put into poetry for his wife:

> "Must ever I be so
>   Yellow and old?" you asked,
> "With living overtaxed,
>   Ugly, and racked with pains?"
> I answered, "Even so,
>   Dearest; yet love remains."

He died in 1957 at his home in Yorkley at the age of 69.

"I know not how the little rills
Are born, nor how the daffodils,
Nor how the steadfast giant hills.

Naught know I of the light fast stored
To fill each golden morrow full;
Naught of those reeds whose whispered word
Turns all the river sorrowfull.

And of the source of mortal breath,
And of the cause of human pain,
And of the lonely house of Death,
And of the life things live again,
With certainty I know but this —

That God's keen arrows cannot miss;
That nothing was and nothing is
Too far or small for Love to kiss.
And when these worlds are drifted dust
About the chariot wheels of fate,
This single knowledge shall, I trust,
Survive the brunt of giant wars,
And when the heavens are desolate
Outlast the ruin of the stars.''

F. W. Harvey's poetry is neglected nowadays. I have met local school-teachers who have not even heard of him. Forest of Dean children should surely be given the opportunity of knowing his poems, even though poetry may not be to everybody's enjoyment. His folk-poems· have music in them. They could be sung to any accompaniment. I know there is enough talent in the Dean for this to be possible, the creation of genuine modern Forest of Dean folk-songs. They could be incorporated in a revived festival of music in the magic and enchantment of the Devil's Chapel in Springtime. Harvey's bugle note again calling us from our drowsing, trumpeting us through beauty to God's side. Why not?

"Lovers goodbye! I cannot stay
To linger out a dusty day,
There is soft sleep beneath the yew
Whose lamps burn red above my head.
I need no ray to light the way —
All ways are ended. I am dead.
'Tis from the grave I call to you,
    Lovers goodbye."

                                    F. W. Harvey.